Veterans' Voices

Helen Aitchison

This book is dedicated to all service personnel past, present and future who have served for Queen and country and who will continue to serve for King and country.

Contents

Foreword

Veterans' Voices was created through the voices of the men and women accessing Operation Veteran and an extra voice of my dad, John.

The idea of the anthology was born through funding secured by The Business Factory, North Tyneside from The National Lottery Community Fund. The grant was awarded to explore creative writing with individuals at Operation Veteran. I had recently set up my own business, Write on the Tyne and felt we could do something bigger than a creative writing class. After managing veteran services in a former role, I had a sense of wanting to share stories far and wide, to educate, raise awareness, celebrate our heroes and commemorate our fallen service people. My desire was to help create a legacy for the many people in this book, but also for other veterans and families of veterans.

The stories in this anthology may be about the military but alongside this, they are stories filled with experiences we all have, whether we have served in the armed forces or not. Themes of adversity, fear and inner strength. Stories of hope, humanity and humour. Messages of friendship, family and love.

I hope *Veterans' Voices* educates you, inspires you and resonates with you in some way.

Profits from the *Veterans' Voices* anthology will be shared between Operation Veteran and Write on the Tyne. Both organisations are community interest companies and not for profit. Any money raised will go back into the community, helping the businesses with their aims of supporting local people.

For more information about the author, Write on the Tyne and Operation Veteran, please visit

www.helenaitchisonwrites.com

www.writeonthetyne.com

www.operationveteran.co.uk.

The Scars of War
Alan Doyle

Name: Alan Doyle
Age: 70 years old
Armed Forces, Regiment / Rank: Territorial Army (1965-70), Northumberland Fusiliers – Lance Corporal. British Army (1970-1980), Gunner, Physical Training Instructor, Acting Sergeant.
Conflicts / Tours served: Northern Ireland (8 Tours), Cyprus
Date entered: 1965
Date left: 1980

My military life started in the TA with the Northumberland Fusiliers, which disbanded in the 1970s. Before embarking on a military career, I worked as an engraver, something I would return to in later life. I enjoyed the TA and progressed into the regular army in 1970, entering the forces as a gunner and serving in this role for three years. I applied to attend a physical training course in the army and qualified after a few years, obtaining a role as a physical training instructor (PTI).

As a PTI, the best posting was to Cyprus in the early 1970s. It was like a three-month holiday. I was my own boss to a degree, so could enjoy myself, exploring a new place in the glorious sunshine. I was like a playboy and everything felt like fun and games, a stark contrast to the time I would spend in my military career in Northern Ireland. In Cyprus, I was 'living it up.' I would participate in scuba diving, parachuting and extreme sports, alongside a good dose of partying. I was very physically fit then and I remember getting a telling off from my boss one day, after going rogue on the sports, freefalling from a plane. He said, "Doyle, next time use a parachute."

My reply was, "I'm a Geordie, what do I want one of them for!" I was young and adventurous and thought I was invincible. We would get up at 5 am, jump and freefall, from planes by 6 am. We would do 5-second delays, 10-second delays, 20-second delays as we progressed through learning the art of parachuting.

Me (early 1970s)

When I was fully qualified at a PTI, we would teach many of the para's and this included a course called P Company. It was a strenuous course with scrutiny, designed by the physical training core and included parachuting. The para's (and the SAS) were the only people who could jump at 600 feet. This was due to the speed at which you would hit the ground from 600 feet and the time needed to release and activate the parachute. The equipment has advanced through the years but there were, as there are still now, major risks. We would teach the para's the skills. Not many people like PTI's, as we could make people do physical activity that may have been a weekly or monthly activity for them, but was daily for us.

Me, right, training soldiers during my time as PTI

During service, every regiment went on a spearhead. This meant that wherever in the world that there were troubles, the spearhead battalion would travel to where they were needed at the time. This included Northern Ireland, even if you may have just recently returned from a tour. Northern Ireland needed extra support during the 70s as the troubles were so bad. I was posted to Northern Ireland each year from 1970-76 with two emergency tours in between. I lost eight friends in Northern Ireland, it was a horrific conflict and I still think about it to this day.

Within the army, another of my roles was as a photographer. It took me to some dark places, disturbing and dangerous sites that stay with me. It was my job and I completed each task, knowing it could save people, including us. However, at times, it felt like my own heart would stop with sadness, anger and fear.

Me (early 1970s)

Northern Ireland (1970s)

We would go on patrol to certain areas and bin lids would be clashing, almighty noises mixed in with dogs barking. It was people alerting terrorists who may have been training in the backyard or the nearby field, that we were there and to take cover. It was a sickness that ran through the houses, the streets, and the communities in some terrorist hot spot areas. Hate, spreading like the air around them. The terrorists would also use violence and threats to take over people's homes, utilising the commandeered house to shoot from. They would fire, leave the house and travel through pre-arranged homes, this would be their escape routes. It made it difficult to spot the terrorists, they were walking in everyday life.

I was in Ireland on the 30th January 1972, Bloody Sunday. Myself and comrades were on the next block of houses in Derry when carnage commenced. The paras involved were inexperienced. They had never been fired at before and hadn't been to Northern Ireland. The way terrorism often happened in dense places, would be that the crowds of people would disperse, coming apart then shots would

Northern Ireland (1970s)

be aimed down the middle of the crowd, at targets. After this, the crowd would close in again, filling the gap so terrorists could not be located and it would be assumed the shots came from the crowd. It was all planned and the para's not being as experienced, did not know this. It led to the death of 14 civilians, through British troops firing into the crowds.

Northern Ireland was war. Not like Afghan or the Falklands, as they didn't wear a uniform. But it was still war and the terrorists would walk the streets when no soldiers were present, dressed in khakis and take photographs for propaganda, used in their own magazines and national newspapers. From 1973 onwards, the terrorists in Northern Ireland began targeting mainland Britain, including the army site where I did my PTI training in Aldershot. They also bombed some pubs in Gilford, where five people were killed, four of which were off-duty soldiers. They bombed Birmingham, Manchester and Liverpool. There was a band of troops travelling down the motorway with horses and a terrorist device was activated, killing 17 soldiers. This psychological warfare technique, when the British troops were in Northern Ireland, meant they worried about their families at home. There weren't any boundaries, there are no boundaries with terrorists.

We had to have our wits about us in Northern Ireland, but we are all human. It was excruciatingly difficult at times and I lost a few of my comrades through impulsive decision-making. A friend of mine, a brilliant soldier, saw something down an alleyway. He went to investigate and it was a suspect rifle behind a dustbin. Naturally, he went to pick up the rifle. It triggered a bomb and killed him. In a split second, the world changed.

When we first went to Northern Ireland, we didn't all have accommodation, and some accommodation was very substandard. We knew we wouldn't be living in The Ritz, but we couldn't live in tents as we would be a target. In a town centre, we would have around eight men patrolling one street and another eight patrolling another street. Some of the soldiers may have been on the street, patrolling for 12-14 hours. They would go and sleep on the stairs in a building basement and the rest would keep patrolling. It was exhausting at times but we never let each other down.

Northern Ireland (1970s)

Northern Ireland (1970s)

The people in Northern Ireland were very kind. They would bring us cups of tea and coffee, soup and sandwiches. They were grateful and frightened. Some weren't as nice, they would spit at us and shout abuse, but they were the minority.

A friend of mine was part of the intelligence group, a team who would pick up information from the regiment before the changeover and new soldiers came out. We shared the same room and were close. He knew all about bomb devices and traps. We were on patrol one day and came across an old building. He was around 50-60 feet ahead of me and he got his torch out to look into the building. The front door was slightly ajar, so he shone his torch through the gap. The torchlight must have activated a sensor in the room and the whole building exploded. Another good guy, gone in a split second. We went to the National Memorial Arboretum in Staffordshire and his name was there, near a newly planted tree. The scars of war never heal. It still hurts now to talk about it.

Northern Ireland (1970s)

Northern Ireland went on for so long and we were governed. Some of this was a good thing, some not so good and when you are out there, witnessing the horror, the terror, the attacks and death, it is hard to understand some of the politics. The terrorists used the dirtiest tactics they could. They would use nail bombs, launch petrol bombs, dropping them from flats above you. They would throw paving slabs, washing machines and TV's from roofs and windows. They would hide bombs in baby's prams. After a while, sniffer dogs were implemented to help detect explosives as there was nowhere the terrorists wouldn't plant them. A mission to kill, maim and destroy.

Northern Ireland (1970s)

For much of my time in Northern Ireland, I would photograph incidents. I was a trained photographer and we needed photos as evidence, intelligence and confirmation of attacks and fatalities. One time there had been an incident in Dungiven, where five terrorists had blown themselves up. I was ordered to go and take photographs of the site and bodies. It was 4 am and off I went, in the cold winter. The explosion had blown all the electrics in the area, so there was no light. The Land Rovers were shining the lights on the area as I took photographs. We couldn't wait for the forensics to arrive so I had to bag the body parts myself. Much of the time, I was in civvy clothes and I remember coming back being covered in blood, soaked through to my skin from my shirt and jeans. There was zero mental health support in those days, I had to get on with it, just like my comrades. Talking about it, much of it sounds like a horror film. I guess it was and we were all cast in the film, but at the end of the day, we didn't take our make-up off, leave the character on set and go to a posh hotel. This was real, it was our lives.

There was a huge hole from the explosion and I took the photos as best I could, returning to my base to process the film. After printing the photographs, I handed them to my superior. He studied the photos and mentioned there were four terrorists in the shots. I corrected him, there were five bodies, not four. He repeated, telling me there were four terrorist's bodies. At the time, one of our soldiers had gone undercover, infiltrating the IRA, trying to get evidence on the terrorists to prevent further destruction. He had been killed, he was one of ours.

In 1976, an incident occurred in South Armagh that I was called out to. There had been an Orange Day Parade, where all the Orangemen would parade and IRA sympathisers would try and prevent it. The Orangemen had gone back to a community hut once the parade was over, had removed their regalia and were playing dominoes and cards together. The Orangemen were all around 85-90 years old. The IRA came, blocked the exits and threw some grenades in before machine-gunning the building. 17 men were murdered. The ammunition technical officer (ATO) had to enter the site, to check there were no bombs left, then I had to go in and photograph the scene.

A few years ago, a social worker came into my shop and we got talking about the army. He asked if I had any counselling after what had happened in the forces. I told him I was almost 70 years old and that was my excuse. But in all seriousness, I told the social worker that we all just had to swallow down the emotion and get on with it. However, even now, telling my story is very emotional for me. Because it was real, it was my life. It isn't a film, or a documentary on TV. It was reality, what I witnessed and what others witnessed. I have never forgotten. At the time there was no dialogue about what you saw, what you had to do and how it made you feel. We would write reports on the incidents of that day. Brutal incidents and gruesome detail documented then filed, emotions filed along with them. You never got any feedback on the reports or questions, especially about how you were managing emotionally.

Sometimes I am in the car or sitting somewhere, perhaps at home and I think about it and what happened in Northern Ireland. I spent a lot of years diving to the floor when I would hear a car backfiring or a loud noise. It was automatic and people would look like I was mad. I did not considered it could have been post-traumatic stress disorder (PTSD), it was just part of my life and part of my life that I never talked about.

When I left the army, I returned to engraving, with my old boss. I worked with them for a few years before deciding to set up my own business, after the seed of the idea was planted by a buyer. The idea stuck and I engaged with a service called Entrust in Byker, that helped set up and support small businesses. Alongside this, I studied a two-year business studies course with Durham University. My business was born and I worked hard to establish it, build a customer base and a positive experience for the clients.

35 years ago, I was making a sign for a friend who opened a florist. My beloved Linda was there and as soon as I saw her, I knew I had to ask her out. She was stunning and I felt giddy with excitement, praying she would be single. I was the world's worst guy for chatting a woman up and Linda seemed shy, like me in lots of ways. Trying to act cool, I asked her to make me some poppy corsages for 11th November. I wanted a posh one for Remembrance Day. She created some and they

were beautiful. I gifted some to the older veterans and they were delighted. I was smitten and asked Linda out. I then found out the 11ᵗʰ November was also Linda's birthday and it seemed like destiny, her special day was a special day for me. Linda accepted my invitation to go on a date and I was beaming. I felt 6'3" tall rather than the actual 5'3" I am in reality!

Linda and me on our wedding day (2006)

Linda had a horse at the time and I had to pass the acceptance test with her first love, her horse. My uncle was a jockey, Willie Snaith, who had won the Northumberland Plate twice and end up being the trainer in Newmarket. This impressed Linda and we became a match made in heaven. After a few dates, I knew it was love and we have been together since, marrying 16 years ago. Linda is the light of my life, we work together at the business and we support one another with everything.

I keep in touch with Jim and visit Operation Veteran when I can and when I'm not working. It is a brilliant service and I have helped with their signage. I am pleased I can contact Jim if needed and the work he and the team do is amazing, a real community asset.

Dedicated to my wife, Linda Doyle

A New Start
Albert

Name: Albert
Age: 82 years old
Armed Forces, Regiment / Rank: British Army, Royal Army Service Core, Driver
Conflicts / Tours served: Borneo, Bahrain, Germany
Date entered: January 1962
Date left: 1968

Before joining the army, at 21 years old, I had learnt the trade of painting and decorating. Life had been challenging for me and I was estranged from my family, with nowhere to turn. I needed something in my life; stability, routine and opportunity. It presented itself via a friend who came home on leave from the army, telling me of how the Royal Army Service Core was the best thing ever. It sounded like an adventure, a great career and a community all in one and I was sold! I travelled to my local recruiting office in Newcastle and enquired about joining up, requesting to be a driver. After sitting a brief exam there and then, I passed before being asked by the recruiting officer when I wanted to start. I advised him I wanted to get away, I had nothing to stay in Newcastle for. His response was, "Tomorrow?"

I settled on the day after that, allowing me to be mentally prepared and ready for a new life. When visiting the army office to swear my oath of allegiance I was greeted by a retired mayor who seemed to be rather tipsy. He looked at me and with a slight slurring of words and perhaps a hiccup or two told me he wished he could swap places with me and do it all again. I had no doubts army life was the path for me.

After a difficult home life and no real place to call home, I found a home in the army and felt the contentment I had been searching for. On entering the army, I began six months of basic training at Buller Barracks in Aldershot. I managed to avoid getting a haircut for three days. My hair was a thick, dark Elvis-style quiff with a 'duck's arse,' at the back and neat sideboards. I had managed to avoid the barbers until my sergeant sent me. Asking for a light trim as I slid onto the barber's chair, he began shaving into my styled hair. Seeing it fall onto my shoulder and floor I quickly asked in a panicked voice, what he was doing. There was nothing light about that trim! He looked at me, sternly and replied that anything under the beret was mine and I could do with it what I pleased. Anything visible outside of the beret, well that was his style. So off it went, cascading onto the floor, my fashionable hairstyle, to be replaced by a crew cut of some sort. I went in like Elvis and came out like Jerry Lewis. It could have been worse!

I was amazed by what was on offer. Of course, we had to learn, obey and work hard as well as keep ourselves and our belongings clean and neat, but there were many elements of the army I had craved in civilian life and found immediately; indoor plumbing and hot showers, laundry facilities and the most wonderful food and plenty of it. I remember being the first up in the mornings, starting my day off with a lovely warm shower, very different from the tin bath from my childhood. Then having a cooked breakfast and a big mug of tea to set me up for the day. It was wonderful and alongside this comforting side, I also made some great friends, the camaraderie feelings as satisfying as the warm, rich meals.

A couple of months into basic training, I commenced training at driving school. I passed my driving test in the army and learnt about the vehicles for a few months before being transferred to air dispatch training at Abingdon for six weeks. Following my completion of this training, I was then posted to Singapore, at RAF Seletar. Singapore was a tropical paradise, more magnificent than I could ever have imagined and our RAF base was sublime. I was assigned to be part of 55 Company Air Dispatch. There were around 100 of us in the unit and 4,000 RAF in the camp. It was phenomenal, with the most amazing facilities. The food was even better than the army food, it was a real delight.

We would work in the mornings for around three to four hours, practicing picking up loads and various other tasks. Then in the early afternoon, we would finish for the day. Usually one or two beers would be consumed in the NAAFI, then it would be time for a nap, or 'gonk,' as we called it. Our alarm at the base was music coming through speakers at 3 pm each day. It was 'The Rhythm of the Rain,' by The Cascades and would gently pipe through the speakers, starting with soft thunder and rain, followed by the bouncy beat and singing. It was sure to wake you up in a good mood, rather than the shock of an abrupt alarm clock or siren. After waking up, we would go down to the Olympic-sized swimming pool, enjoying the cool water and a little exercise. Following this, we would return for dinner, then perhaps a film at the cinema on site, finishing the day off with a few beers in the NAAFI. It was heaven!

The first week of basic training, Aldershot (1962).
Me, back row, first left

I also completed jungle survival courses throughout my time in Singapore, which were fantastic. We were required to complete these as we were part of the flight crew and it was essential we knew what to do if we were involved in a plane crash, assuming we survived the initial crash. We mixed with other regiments for this, including US forces and it was always great fun, even considering the unpredictability of the jungle.

In December 1962, I had been out in Singapore for around four to five months and the Brunei Revolt happened. I was a duty driver, travelling from one camp to another. There was radio silence and my role was to deliver messages between the camps. I saw the armed Gurkhas boarding a plane on the day the revolt began and on my return to camp, the RSM told us we were going to Brunei the next day.

RAF Combat Survival School, Singapore (1965).
Me, front row, third from left.

"But there is a war there!" was my initial response, having yet to serve in conflict and being used to the surroundings of RAF Seletar. We were ordered to go to Brunei the following day, by which time the revolt was over. However, we did witness the damage and that evening the airport manager told us of the devastation that had occurred in just a few days. I remained in Brunei, for around four to six weeks in airport security, meeting, packing and unpacking the aircrafts. Following Brunei, I was posted to Labuan Island to set up a R&R (rest and recuperation) base which was wonderful and proved to be another beautiful place.

A memorable experience I had in the forces was a driving posting with a medical team. When we were in Labuan, I was on stand down from air dispatch. We had been working really hard for a week and a little time off was due. Some of us were sitting, chatting and a sergeant major walked over. He looked

at me and stated he needed a volunteer to drive a medical
team around. The criteria required was a non-smoking, non-
swearing driver who didn't get drunk. I fitted the bill, well
mostly! I enquired what would happen if I didn't volunteer
and I was promptly told by the sergeant major that he would
make my life hell. So through gritted teeth, I agreed and left
the next day.

Surrender Point, Labuan Island (1963)

It turned out to be a brilliant posting and the initial job of
a fortnight turned into four months. The role was to drive
Colonel Boyle, who was the highest ranking doctor on the
island. Alongside the colonel was his Lieutenant Colonel
McFarren, two sergeants and a corporal. They were excep-
tional people and it was a fantastic few months. One time the
colonel asked me to salute for him. His vehicle was a magnet
to people who wanted to see the colonel and show appreciation. He was sick of dropping his paperwork as we drove, to

respond to all who respected him and saluted him. I advised them I couldn't salute back, after all they were saluting him and not myself. He looked at me pleading with the fact he had a speech to make that evening and couldn't be distracted by saluting to folk every 10 seconds. He pointed out he was of the highest rank on the island and it was an order. So I did it, returning many salutes as we drove to a myriad of confused faces, wondering who I was and what I was doing! I came a cropper when I saw a regimental sergeant major approaching. He straightened up, growing a few inches and my stomach dropped as it registered what was going to happen. Sure as predicted, the sergeant major saluted and I quickly returned the salute, knowing I was in a no-win situation. On my arrival back at the unit, I was washing the vehicle and heard the sergeant major screaming, "YOU!" before I saw him.

Labuan (1964)

I received the biggest scolding of my life but it was soon intervened by Colonel Boyle who went on to apologise to me for ordering me to salute. Colonel Boyle wanted me to stay longer, he was wonderful and they were a brilliant bunch, who felt like family. They respected me and made me feel part of their team, including trips to the Happy Bar, a local drinking haunt. It was an unforgettable time in my army career that I still think of so fondly. I stayed three years in the far east and it was the most amazing three years of my life.

After three phenomenal years, I was posted to the Middle East in 1965. For me, this posting felt like the opposite end of the spectrum to remarkable Singapore. Just before the Middle East, I had returned to the UK to Bordon in Hampshire. It thought it should have been called 'Boring,' not Bordon and I applied for an emergency posting, in an attempt to get away from Bordon. A transfer landed my way in Bahrain, with my O.C. advising me, "You're not going to like it." I can't say he didn't warn me!

My posting in Bahrain was a year long. The silver lining was that I met my wife, Christine, out in Bahrain. She was working in the pay office and needed an escort. I became her driver, transporting her around the married quarters to complete various procedures and checks. During my year in Bahrain, I was sent to Aden. This was a year before the Northumberland Fusiliers and others were killed. We were there because of the Sheik. He was Sunni and the majority of people were Shia. The Shiek was in control and had the Americans and us there as a protectorate. It felt risky and I never felt comfortable for long in Bahrain.

The rest of my service was in Germany. I remember arriving on January 2nd, 1967 and wow, was it cold! This was coming from a North East England man, where it is never very warm, even in the height of summer. It was made even colder by the fact I hadn't seen snow for four years, having served in Singapore and the Middle East. Once I acclimatised, Germany was ok and I enjoyed my time there.

I left the army after six years. I was offered a promotion but I had always been content as a squaddie; happy and grateful in my position. On leaving, Christine and I got married. She didn't want me to remain in the army and I understood. Christine's father had been in the army, achieving a high rank. He was a great man, working in bomb disposal. He served 33 years then worked at Scotland Yard on the bomb squad. When I left the army, I worked on the buses, continuing my love of driving. However, I didn't enjoy it and ended up back in my school-leaving trade of painting and decorating. Christine and I went on to have two children, a boy and a girl, now aged 55 and 47 years old.

Around 15 years ago, I became involved with military life again, through various associations. It started with a local Saturday Club at the RBL after being invited by a friend of mine. I really enjoyed it and that's where I met two men who became great friends, Billy Ness and Jim Cauldwell. I returned the next week and it developed into a regular event, connecting with the group over shared experiences. That feeling of camaraderie was back. Sadly, as time went on, the numbers got lower with people passing. I am a member of the Malaya and Borneo Association and the Parachute Regiment Association, The Royal Engineers, The Royal Army Service Core Association, the RBL and I come to Operation Veteran whenever I can. I've met some amazing people through the Associations, years may pass but there is always an understanding between servicemen.

Up until around 18 months ago, I was a friend and carer for Billy Ness. Billy was a legendary veteran in the North East, who was known throughout the country and further afield for his time in the Second World War. We travelled to Normandy seven years ago for the 70th anniversary and again two years for the 75th anniversary. The trips were magnificent and Billy had a fantastic time. He was surrounded everywhere we went,

Billy Ness, RIP. A true hero and friend.

with people thanking him and wanting their photograph taken with him. Rightly so, he was a hero and tragically lost

120 of his comrades on D-Day, all those years ago in 1944. Time may have passed but the memories hadn't. It was an honour to accompany him, support him and to be his friend. Billy sadly passed 18 months ago, aged 94 years old. I treasure our time together and cherish the memories. He is often in my thoughts. I miss him dearly and my life has been enhanced by knowing him, even though I wish he had been in my life longer.

Me (left) with my friend, Sergeant Major Jim Cauldwell

Dedicated to Billy Ness.

Direction
Andrew (Andy) Newman

Name: Andrew (Andy) Newman
Age: 38 years old
Armed Forces, Regiment / Rank: British Army, First Battalion Coldstream Guards; Guardsman
Conflicts / Tours served: Northern Island, Iraq and Afghanistan
Date entered: 2001
Date left: Feb 2014

I'm dyslexic and struggled as a child. The condition wasn't recognised back in the 1980s and school, therefore was challenging. Adding to my difficulties were several bullies, who targeted me at school, both physically and emotionally abusing me. Unsurprisingly, school wasn't a place of learning, socialising and positive memories for me.

Despite my adversity, I still achieved grades and went on to college. However, my family couldn't afford a computer and college became too much of a challenge for me. My confidence was low and I felt I had no direction. College could have been a new start, away from the bad memories of school but it wasn't working and I felt crushed, my self-esteem disintegrating despite my hopes.

By the age of 17, as I struggled on at college, I felt like a hamster on a wheel, going nowhere. I was like the famous Scooby Doo character, Shaggy; demotivated, unfocused, a liability and always eating junk food! One day it struck me, like the dart impaling the bullseye, that I had two options. One, that I could continue being like Shaggy and ultimately, go nowhere. Or I could take control, muster up all my courage and take a leap of faith, that could change my life for the better.

My leap of faith was the military and I thought that joining the army could give me that direction, motivation and the purpose I was so desperately searching for. The army could change my life and perhaps make me as tough as the lads who bullied me at school. I joined the army and ended up staying for 13 years.

Me in Northern Ireland
(2002)

When I entered the army and throughout my time in the forces, I wasn't interested in rank and promotion. I didn't want to be a career soldier, I just wanted a purpose. I was one week past my 18th birthday when I was posted to Northern Ireland, fresh out of basic training. There were only three Coldstream Guards that made it through training and Northern Ireland needed soldiers. There was a guy who was 17 years old (the same age as me at the time) and an older guy, who was around the age of 21. The sergeant ordered the older guy to his office and informed him he would be posted to Northern Ireland, as he was the only soldier over 18 years old. However, on the bright side, he would get two weeks off before his deployment. He replied to the sergeant, like the class snitch, advising him that if I also got two weeks off, I would then be over 18 years old and could go to Northern Ireland. I saw the funny side of it, this was a classic example of army banter. Consequently, I ended up in Northern Ireland, where I stayed for just under two years. During my time in Northern Ireland, the war in Iraq started.

On return to the UK, I was posted to Aldershot. During this time, I met my wife on a night out. We were smitten and got engaged quickly. I didn't want to leave the army yet, so continued in my service and around three months after I got back from Iraq, we got married. I then thought it would be worth staying in the army for a year or so, for my career but also once you join, there is a loyalty that becomes as important as breathing at times.

About a year into my marriage, conflict in Afghanistan had been going on for about five years and whilst I was only a small cog in a big system, I felt obliged and wanted to go on tour. I was posted to Afghanistan with the mindset that I would leave the army when I returned. At the time I had a young daughter and another on the way, I wanted to be with my loved ones and settle into family life. I missed the birth of my second child whilst I was in Afghanistan. It was hard, not being there for my wife. My gran also died the week before my second daughter was born, which was another blow. It was hard; loyalties and duty torn, in conflict themselves. My wife became poorly after the birth of our second child, so I came home on leave for a short time, before returning to Afghanistan once again.

My wife, Claire and I

It was tough for my wife and children when I was in the forces. Families were never really talked about and I know at times, it was scary, worrying and difficult for my wife. She tried living in married quarters but it simply wasn't for her. It isn't just the deployment for tours, it's the months of regimented training needed to prepare as a soldier, which meant so little family time. The forces are a culture within itself and it isn't for everyone. It can be lonely for spouses and more lonely in the barracks, away from their community, networks and support. My wife comes from a close-knit family, she wanted to be around them and it was a relief for me when I was away, knowing she had loved ones nearby.

But it was still hard, emotionally. I missed my wife and children, home comforts and routines. I was still young and going to conflict, I knew there would be casualties and fatalities. I knew that I could be one of those statistics. It was real and raw.

Much of the time on tour, it could be excruciatingly boring. Your posting meant that you would do the same patrols, day in, day out. You would walk down the same road, pass the same rock. Monotony, like groundhog day. It could be tedious and make the void of home seem even bigger. It was a cut that never healed fully. It felt like this 95% of the time but we had to be ready, prepared and sharp like a racehorse ready to take off from the stalls for that 5%. The days would be long, exasperating and frustrating. Then as quick as lightning, someone would say something that would have us all belly laughing. A one liner, a story or a joke that would be the exact medicine we needed right there and then. Even if it was from someone who you clashed with, it was sustenance for the soul and made the tedium so much more bearable. Humour got us through so much.

Of course, there is the not-so boring and not-so-humorous side of a conflict, as we all know. The side which involves casualties, fatalities and horror. Once there was a riot in Iraq following some soldiers being captured. Petrol bombs and rioting occurred all day with shots fired. That evening, the roll call started and some of the team were missing. They were wounded and in hospital. Times like that were a too close for comfort, a reminder that we weren't invincible.

Another memorable incident happened in Afghanistan. By the time I was deployed, I was trained in infantry regimental signals. There had been an attack and a large number of Afghans had been killed. Some of us were asked to go and guard the tent that contained all the bodies. It was an eerie experience. The helicopters arrived to take the dead away and we were asked to put the body bags onto the helicopter. In those situations, your mind plays tricks on you. I can still recall the feeling as I carried the body bags. Sweating and my heart racing, wondering is the guy actually dead. Panicking in case he wasn't. Ruminating over what had happened, who was he? Whose son? Father? The reality of war, there in the masses on the ground. We had supported our injured comrades out in conflict, patched them up and helped them back to base. But not knowing what was inside those body bags, my mind became the enemy.

Many of my tours felt like tipping scales; the extremely bad and the extreme good. I remember the views of the mountains in Afghanistan. Such beauty in nature and despite the horror around them, they stood, in spectacular view for all to see. At times, when life felt emotionally and physically exhausting, when our minds felt like the enemy, we would stand with a cup of coffee and look at that view. Those magnificent mountains calmed us, like a comforting embrace, even if just for 10 seconds.

When I returned from Afghanistan I was posted to Catterick. This base was the closest to home, meaning a better work-life balance. My wife had been poorly and it was important that I had a steady job but that I was available to support her as she recovered. I was assigned a post in the training school at Catterick. However, I was injured on a training exercise and was offered a desk job, where I remained for a couple of years before leaving the army in 2014. There are people from the forces I still keep in touch with, mainly on social media. Experiences we will never forget, forever connected.

When I left the army, after going in to 'find myself,' ironically, I struggled with who I was. The army had defined me through my lack of direction and the process of training. I had become what the army wanted and needed me to be. Outside of the army, I wasn't sure who Andy was. I needed a new identity in civvy street as Andy, the husband and the father. I decided to go to University to study history. I had been studying a little when I had my desk job in the army so it felt like a natural progression. As I studied and adjusted to civvy street, I became more concerned and frustrated with the lack of support for people coming out of the forces. Granted, it has improved greatly from what was available decades ago but issues around veterans with mental ill health, suicide rates, the number of soldiers in the criminal justice system and the sheer lack of understanding around the support needed, even at local levels concerned me.

Me, in Afghanistan

I remember being turned down for social housing as my wife was told she was intentionally homeless after leaving the house in the army married quarters. This wasn't uncommon back then, across the country. There was a deep lack of knowledge about the needs of veterans. I recall a conversation with my aunt where I was complaining about it all. She simply told me I should do something about it and go into politics. I dismissed it, thinking no one would want to listen to me, a worn-out soldier. The drip of curiosity wouldn't stop and the more I contemplated it, the more I thought that perhaps I could make a difference and be an advocate.

Almost nine years ago, I emailed the Labour Party, asking to be involved and before I knew it, I was elected as a local councillor. Although I went into the party with a focus on veterans, I quickly found I was able to attempt to influence and shape

Me, in Basra, Iraq

other areas of politics and social needs. I am chair of the housing committee and part of the education committee. As someone who has dyslexia and didn't get help at school, my aim is to raise awareness and support provisions locally and nationally.

I continued to raise the profile of veterans. North Tyneside does a brilliant job to support veterans and improve services. This started with Cllr Gary Bell, who was the armed forces champion before me and the Mayor, Norma Redfearn. I have spoken at political events and within the community. There have been national changes for the better, but as a country, we have a long way to go and I want to be part of this positive change. I enjoy my job, I'm passionate about it and I hope I can continue to make a small difference for a long time. Austerity impacted everyone, including veterans and times will get harder. We need those specialist services, we need to support our veterans in civvy street. I will keep campaigning for their voice. It isn't about pushing politics onto people, it's about trying to listen, trying to make a difference and I hope I can do that for a long time.

Dedicated to my wife, Claire.

Lifelong Honour
Andrew (Andy) Owens

Name: Andrew (Andy) Owens
Age: 80 years old
Armed Forces, Regiment / Rank: British Army, Royal Artillery, Gunner.
Tours / Conflicts served: Malaya, Borneo, Germany, Northern Ireland
Date entered: December 1960
Date left: 1974

I wanted to join the army since I can remember and I felt like the luckiest lad in North Shields, when I joined the Cadets, aged 12. Throughout my whole military career, I wore the same camp badge in my beret, The Royal Artillery badge. It is a part of my heart, my soul and has been a huge element of my life, both in and out of the armed forces.

At 18 years old, I joined the regular army. It was Boxing Day 1960 when I signed up and I began my career, completing my basic training at Oswestry Barracks, Shropshire. It was strange being away from home but I had some insight into army training expectations, after spending several years in the cadets. At times the routine, the discipline and the self-motivation could be a challenge but it was a challenge I loved. The military was my natural fit. After training, I just wanted to get out into the world.

I was posted to Hong Kong, where I spent three years. It was phenomenal! I was just a kid, it was the first time I had ever been on a plane and out of the country. An adventure lay ahead that made me feel like I could take on the world and I wanted to learn, develop and experience all that life in the army could offer me!

Hong Kong was wonderful; the culture, the people, the whole experience. It was a place that felt advanced to the UK in many ways and the sights were magnificent. There were no conflicts in Hong Kong at the time, but the possibility of unrest with the communists. We were posted to be there on standby for any issues and riots that may start. We had some memorable times in Hong Kong. We would be asked to volunteer to guard the racecourse on racing days. My hand would shoot up at the speed of light to offer my assistance. It was a brilliant job and the atmosphere was electric with serious gambling at stake. There was a big gambling culture in Hong Kong, at times I thought they would bet on a fly!

I remember taking in the atmosphere, the sights, sounds and hustle and bustle of Hong Kong. I recall getting suits and shoes handmade before returning home. I felt like a film star in my tailored suit, made to measure, finished off with matching, hand-crafted shoes. They were so cheap and I dread to think how much you would have paid for the beautiful garments in London. I certainly felt special returning home on leave.

Me (right), in Hong Kong (1963)

Whilst in Hong Kong, we also took part in Queen Elizabeth II's birthday parade. It was a colourful parade, in our best kit with all the regiments in their uniforms and the locals coming along to watch, cheering and smiling. We would also travel out to Hong Kong island and they had the most stunning beaches, like in the movies, endless blue sea that the sun reflected onto and golden beaches that almost screamed for you to lie on. It was a beautiful sight, etched on my mind forever.

In 1965, I was posted to Malaya. At the time President Sukarno of Indonesia was on the move, trying to dominate neighbouring countries and mobilising a series of aggressive foreign policies. It was an uncertain time and my first real experience of conflict, as Hong Kong had felt like a three year holiday in many ways.

I was in Malaya for around six months and from there, I was posted to Borneo for six months after a very short training stint in jungle school. Although nothing could have prepared me for the Borneo jungle! Borneo was a big eye-opener. On arrival, we had to set up a camp. We dug underground, creating a shelter with an overhead structure covered with material. We used to hear and see the rats scurrying over the top of the shelter. Barb wire and traps were strategically placed around the parameter of the camp, protecting us and defending our territory.

The weather was stifling and we sweated non-stop, not just with the humid climate, but our layers of clothing and the weight of our weapons and kit, adding to our draining, heat-induced fatigue. The darkness of the jungle was phenomenal and the sounds from the animals became our own, private wildlife concert. Some of the noises the birds made were like nothing I had heard before and they almost sounded like humans as they chatted after dark. It took some getting used to, to identify it was an animal and not a human. We would conduct shifts of two-hour watches through the night, on standby for predators. With the pitch black darkness, the songs and the jungle movements of the animals, it was a nerve-testing shift.

The animals in the jungle were almost as frightening

predators as humans. One time, we were driving along in Borneo on a dirt track and I saw a large log in the road. This could have been a trap, where the enemy tries to get you to leave your vehicle and move the log, before attacking. We drove right up to the log, slowly, looking around for any possible enemy. Then right before my eyes, the log moved. It was the most enormous snake!

On return to the UK, my next posting abroad was in Germany, in 1966. We were stationed at a base in Northern Germany, about 10 miles from what was left of Bergen Belsen concentration camp. One day I went to Belsen. It was extremely eerie and disturbing, with evidence of mass graves concreted over with memorials placed on top. Over 50,000 people died at Belsen and it was beyond my comprehension to understand what happened there, just two decades earlier. A fellow soldier met his future wife out in Germany. At the time we were posted, they were dating and we asked what it had been like during the Second World War. She had been a young girl then and they were told they weren't allowed to talk about it. All civilians were warned they would go to prison or worse if they were caught talking about Belsen. It was minimised, controlled and people were programmed to say nothing, ask nothing and almost not think about it. They were frightened to speak up in case they were also punished or killed.

I completed a medical in the army after my return from Germany and I was classed as unfit for travel abroad. I was devastated and was advised I could work in the depot on dispatch. We called this 'blanket shuffling,' as basically it meant working in the warehouse dishing out blankets, clothing and toiletries. I was very disgruntled, thinking I could work in a factory in civvy street doing that. At the time Northern Ireland was having troubles and they needed more soldiers. My commander told me I could go as it wasn't abroad, so I jumped at the chance.

I was posted to Maze Prison, an old RAF base that was used from 1971 until 2000 to house paramilitary prisoners and is now a museum. Although I only spent six months in Northern Ireland, it was a long and disturbing six months. We were there to try and prevent the conflict between Catholics and Protestants. It was an awful place and an awful time. I remember one of the most disturbing things about Northern Ireland was that it felt like a "normal" place in so many ways. The area, the streets, houses, shops. People doing their daily lives to a degree, as much as they could. We would be patrolling past shops, like those at home in North Shields and we would see everyday life that I associated with my home-town. Much of the area didn't look like a war zone. In a way, this made it more disturbing.

The sinister side wasn't in sight. People in buildings opened fire, bombs going off in front of you as you travelled in your vehicle down the road. Buses blowing up, the constant threat of your vehicle being the next target. Sometimes we would be driving in armoured vehicles, pigs as we called them, to try and remain safer. The destruction was like a horror film. The constant rioting and kids who were growing up seeing conflict as normal. It was awful and by far the worst conflict I served in. I had comrades who were killed there. Northern Ireland's troubles lasted 32 years, an atrocity, it felt like such a waste.

We have an Artillery day every year and I visit National Arboretum, Staffordshire, where many Northern Ireland lads have a memorial. I have sat there, reflecting on numerous occasions over the years.

On my return from Northern Ireland, in 1972, I worked in the base depot for a few years before retiring from the army in 1974. I learnt a plethora of knowledge in the army and had experiences that I never thought possible; good and bad. I learnt about strength of character, determination, friendship and the importance of doing, not just saying.

During my time in the military, I received my general service medal and had clasps from my various postings in conflict. I felt a massive pride in my achievements and what we had accomplished as a team. My clasps signified Malaya and Borneo and Northern Ireland. Over 30 years after the Malaya conflict ended, all British veterans serving in operations in Malaya/Malaysia between 1957 – 1966 were awarded a separate medal, called the Pingat Jasa Malaysia Medal. It was offered by the Malaysian Government as a thank you and a massive honour to receive.

After leaving the forces, I adjusted to civvy street. At first it was strange, as I'm sure most veterans find, but I got into work easily. I worked at Formica, J&J Fashion and then I ended up working in psychiatry for about eight years. Myself and others had visited St Nicholas's psychiatric hospital in Newcastle. It was like a learning visit for several people who may be interested in working there. Only a few of us decided it could be for us by the end of the afternoon. I had some experience in the forces of how people managed their mental well-being and had seen people struggle. Alongside this, I wanted to try to help and support ill individuals. People have hard times, problems and trauma, I had seen my own share of this in the forces.

St Nicholas's was a great place to work. I helped with activities, monitoring the patient's wellbeing and ensuring daily life was as normal as possible for them. I assisted with mealtimes, medication, washing and dressing. There were many unwell individuals there but I always found that chatting with people was the best medicine. A bit of kindness, understanding, compassion and humanity. It goes a long way. I studied for qualifications at St. Nicholas's and tried to make a difference in the patients' lives, even if only a small one. Sometimes it would involve taking patients on trips, many just wanted the most basic of outings that we all take for granted. I also took someone to get electroconvulsive therapy (ECT) once, which was unpleasant to see.

Medicine and treatment for people with mental ill health have got much better over the years but I still think someone listening and understanding means the world.

Alongside my work after leaving the forces, I met my partner, Dorothy. We have been together for 30 years and she has been part of my military life outside of the army. Dorothy had a son, who tragically died young. However, we have two wonderful grandsons, Karl and Mark, who we are very proud of.

Dorothy and me at Buckingham Palace

I keep active, including being chairman of the North Tyneside Royal Artillery. I am also part of the Elswick All Arms Association and participate in selling the Poppy Appeal each year. I have featured in their advertising, including being part of the Royal British Legion Poppy Appeal, a 70 years plus campaign, with other veterans of various ages. Selling the poppy locally, I have raised some large funds over the years. It gives me enormous pride and I know it makes a big difference. I also enjoy chatting with people when selling, raising awareness and sometimes I see other local veterans, hear their stories and get a chance to reminisce whilst raising money. It always feels like home, to hear about the military. Even though people have served in different conflicts and different decades, there is an understanding. Brothers in arms.

Me during the Poppy Appeal (2021), magazine feature

I've been to Buckingham Palace two times and met King Charles and Camila Queen Consort, during the Poppy

Appeal campaign. The story was also featured in Hello Magazine. One lady involved had been selling the Poppy since the 1940s. It was magnificent on the day. We were all meeting people, being looked after and getting our photographs taken. At one point, we walked to another room and were greeted by some people in the doorway. I assumed they may have been staff, perhaps butlers, or the catering staff or housekeeping. We all shook hands with them and mutual thanks were exchanged. A minute or so later, another Poppy appeal campaign person asked me if I shook hands with the people we had just passed. I said yes and he asked if I realised who it was. I was oblivious, but it had been Dame Judy Dench! Apparently, Camilla had a book club function after our event and famous people were waiting to be part of it. Here I was thinking they were butlers and house help! It was the most wonderful day and another proud, memorable moment in my life.

Poppy Appeal advert (2021)

I participate in local parades and thoroughly enjoy connecting with my comrades and commemorating our fallen soldiers. It means a lot to me to show respect throughout the year and at organised events. I help out with military funerals, offering support, advice and presence on the day. I have travelled locally and beyond, across the country to be there at one of our comrades funerals. It's respect and importance to the families. Those lost are part of my family; my military family.

Poppy Appeal, Buckingham Palace (2021), magazine feature

I attend Operation Veteran as much as I can. It's an amazing place and I have made some wonderful friends. It's welcoming, warm and there is always a cuppa, food and a smile. The team has helped out some veterans in real trouble; homeless, lonely and hungry veterans. There is always someone to ask for advice and always a laugh. Places like Operation Veteran are the heartbeat of the community.

Comradeship is the thing that stands out in my mind from the army. Even after decades, the link, the connection, it remains and I'm honoured to be part of it.

Dedicated to Jim Owens.

Determination of the Human Spirit
Anthony

Name: Anthony

Age: 39 years old

Armed Forces, Regiment / Rank: British Army, Royal Electrical Mechanical Engineers, Craftsman

Date entered: 2000

Date left: 2004

I can't pinpoint why, but I had always envisaged becoming a soldier. Maybe it was a desire to escape my own childhood, or a way to feel a part of something, but I always seemed to know that I would be destined to wear that uniform.

As a child, when people asked me what I wanted to be when I was older, I would always say, "To be in the army." I was drawn to the forces, compelled to be part of it. I even referred to coming home with a flag on my coffin. Though at the time, I had no real understanding of the impact or the sacrifice that would have meant.

I left school and went straight into the 'man's army.' At the time, aged 16, my mother had to sign consent. She only agreed to allow me to join the army if I signed up for a trade. I reluctantly chose mechanics as a way to ensure my enlistment, thinking this could be an option for a career both in the forces and in civvy street. Growing up in the 1990s, there wasn't a boy my age alive who hadn't pinned posters of hot hatches and outrageous supercars on his wall! Mechanics was definitely better than nothing.

Me, aged 16

I didn't go to the academies, where I would complete basic training and an apprenticeship. Instead, I went straight into the deep end, with mainly older soldiers to start my basic training at Pirbright Barracks, Woking. We completed training in the old WWII war sheds, with 30 of us in a room. I had to grow up pretty quickly, being shouted at all day, every day! Physically I was fit, having played sport at school but I was still a child and had to catch up to the levels of the 'men,' fast. My age was not an excuse whilst standing to attention in a platoon of men. I managed to survive and even went on to start enjoying it.

There were funny times and hard times, but lots of laughs. I made friends in basic training. Some soldiers were almost double my age and saw it as their last chance. They took it more seriously. For me, I was growing up as well as learning discipline, respect, motivation and routine.

Comrades became friends and family. We only had each other in those very intensive months and had to learn to be each other's support, each other's crutch in life or death situations. At the age of 16 years old, I learnt how to kill before learning how to pay a bill. Each month we would be paid by the army and all of our accommodation was covered, including our food and utilities. It was a wage with no outgoings to worry about.

After basic training of four months, I went on to trade training to be a mechanic at the school of Electrical and Mechanical Engineers (SEME), Bordon. It was crucial training across various formats and machines. I had originally wanted to be a Para, so during my training, I went down that path, at 3 Para's detachment, Colchester.

Going into my trade, I ended up spending a lot of time in the classroom whilst my comrades were out on detachments, travelling the world. Some were in Ireland, Norway and Iraq, I was in a classroom. I struggled, wanting to be let loose in the world, to explore, experience and grow. I wasn't enjoying army life as I felt I was just in the classroom constantly.

I grew disheartened towards my service when I found that between the ages of 16-18, time served was classed as for 'Queen and country,' so did not count officially regarding time served, pensions etc. At 21, we got our career stamp and could sign off from the forces or sign up again for longer service. I ended up signing myself out of the army thinking I could make my millions outside of the forces, doing private military as a close protection officer. I was still a child but had big dreams and thought as a bodyguard, I would be rich and travel the world. I had friends in the industry and they encouraged me to fly out, claiming I would get work.

When I was in the forces, there were no real conflicts in the world at the time. Very few of us had experiences of war and death. People didn't know anyone who had killed another person. The reality of defending and fighting in a war wasn't our army life reality at the time. We thought we would do tours of Cyprus or visit the army skiing hotels, over 3,000 miles away in the Middle East.

Me, as a young craftsman

I left, to try and make a difference in the world but had no idea what life had in store for me. I flew out to the Middle East and gained work as a close protection officer. However, after three months, the bubble had completely burst and evaporated. I was a young man who thought I could make it big.

Yet the true reality was neither glamorous nor safe. There would be no flag draped across your coffin, it was big boy's rules, with no one was sharing the rules with you, never mind playing by them.

It is hard enough with backup in the military, but in close protection, you have no team. No one to protect you. You were going in as a mercenary, providing a security role without the team of expert intelligence, protection and weapons. There were no sophisticated communication techniques, a lack of chain of command and only small teams that you may have met just once. I lied to my mother, not telling her the reality. It wasn't the military and there were stories on the news about kidnaps, beheadings and people going missing. I got out as quick as I could but I did go back over the year, working mainly in Iraq. It was sad, Iraq used to be a lovely country with landmarks and designer shops. It was all rubble and people's lives had been destroyed, communities ruined. There were times we were targets and colleagues in our teams and other private companies were attacked and killed.

People in the forces, people in the private military they can get stuck with their former role, their identity. Adjusting can be hard and people go back to what their comfort is, their security blanket, somewhere they feel accepted. Acceptance, even with massive risk. Camaraderie does that to you. The understanding, the empathy, the place, the routine. People who are like you and sometimes the risk of death is tolerable for all of that.

When I first left private military, I returned home to the North East. I started working on the fishing boats. My grandfather used to work on fishing boats, relocating from Scotland years ago. Fishing soon became a difficult industry as disputes with Europe escalated. I had a child at the time and pressures to provide for my family, so I returned to security, working locally. Door supervising and looking after bands and celebrities constituted most of my work. It was nice to be back in the 'trade,' on safe ground and close to my family. But it felt like I needed a little more.

I always had an interest in healthcare and medicine, so I began a course in first responder training. It was brilliant and once I completed the course, I went on to do further training, learning all of the time. I ended up working in ambulances, travelling to different places in the world. It felt like a dream and something that gave me the buzz that I first got when I joined the army as a 16-year-old. I progressed onto a role as an NHS Operations Manager, servicing eight hospitals across the North East of England. It worked out well, I could do the job and also some private bodyguarding work at the time. I travelled with famous golfers on the European Golf Tour. It was amazing and I managed to be part of this tour for over a decade.

Five years ago, I had another child with a new partner. My life had been transient, moving around the world, getting the odd job and leaving for another role in a different country at any point. I saw so many men in the private military world get stuck in a system where the big money pays for what has become a lavish lifestyle. Families at home who have had the best and are used to the best, while the man works away in risky conditions, away from home for the big bucks. Keeping the lifestyle going, the large house and new car, the best of the best. I saw so many marriages and relationships fall apart because they were always separated or on their return home, it became evident that it wasn't just the distance in miles between them. Lots of colleagues were older men who never had a long-term relationship. They may have had the money, but when it comes down to it, money can't buy love, well not lasting love anyway. Many had nothing else but work. Their only purpose was an escape in a way but it always felt to me that they were dead men walking.

When you have commitments at home and you've seen how easy relationships fail, you want to try your best. I tried my best, sadly it didn't work out but at the time, I tried to keep my family together. I kept leaving private security and going back to it when the money was there, in between relationships. I have four children with four different women, my oldest child being 21 years old, whom I only met when she was 16 years old, not knowing she was mine. I have a 15-year-old boy, a 9-year-old girl and a 4-year-old boy.

Seven years ago, I had a child who passed away. He was born into intensive care and we were told he wouldn't survive 24 hours. He held on, refusing to give up, for five and half months. He was born with under-developed lungs and they began failing him as his body grew. We were told by the doctors that he wouldn't make it and he would begin suffering if we didn't act now. It was the most difficult time of my life and each moment of the day I seemed to pray for a miracle. The miracle never came and we had to let our baby go, after five and a half months of him fighting his own battle and us wishing with every cell in our body that he could be well. My partner at the time couldn't be there but the military teaches you to never leave anyone dying alone, we fight to the death for each other. I fought even harder when it was my own flesh and blood.

When the time came, I sat holding my son as he slipped away from me, forever. He looked into my eyes as if to say thank you. At the time I shed no tears and it was such a strange feeling to be in that position. Maybe it's the military training that makes us so good at being able to act without emotion and react on autopilot. It is a protection mechanism. But when it is your flesh and blood, you cannot pretend you are ok, well not for long anyway. After we lost our son, I tried to hold it all together and be the man I thought I needed to be. Support and carry my partner and our family. Inside I felt like I was crumbling, like wood foundations in a rotting building. Grief was consuming me, gnawing away, biting at my soul and tearing chunks from my heart.

I suppressed my grief, sadness and pain until it boiled over and I developed PTSD. I would have flashbacks and nightmares about my son but also everything else I had seen in the private military and things since, like relationship breakdowns. It all melted together, polluting my mind. I have struggled for the last seven years with my mental health. As soon as I lost my son and realized I couldn't keep him alive, everything else I had witnessed and suppressed came bursting out of the box I had firmly put it in. It was like an explosion, all the memories forcing themselves out at once and I didn't know how to ask for help.

Shortly after the death of my son, I was diagnosed with cancer. I was only in my early 30s. I remember the day the doctor said it was cancer. She empathetically asked if I was ok as I didn't react. I said "Yes," knowing I had come to find out if I had cancer or not. If she had told me I was pregnant, I would have had the shock of my life and she would have seen more of a reaction! As soon as I was told I had cancer, I vowed to never give my illness the energy it tried to take from me. The murderous poison, growing in my body, wouldn't get me. I wouldn't let it and I promised myself I wouldn't be defeated.

I received treatment for my cancer and refused to let it conquer me. I wouldn't let myself and my family focus on the mental impact, instead diverting my energy into fighting the physical war it inflicted on my body. Six years ago, I defeated it. However, over a year ago I started to not feel myself and had a massive lack of energy. I went to the doctors and it transpired, after testing that I had cancer again. I had a 20cm tumor that was cutting my kidney off and blocking my heart. I was booked in for emergency surgery the next day. A stent was placed in my kidney, which had collapsed. The stent worked and then I began treatment, three separate chemotherapy treatments, 24 hours a day for three months. I told people I had already beaten the current cancer manifesting in my body, I wouldn't give up and give in, just like I hadn't the first time round. The chemo was brutal but my refusal to surrender helped me get through. That positive attitude. I remember sitting in the ward, during the pandemic lockdown, with other patients. The patients who got up and ate, showered and went for their paper – were the ones who walked out at the end. The determination of the human spirit.

I have made a few attempts to take my life over the years. It is strange as I was determined for cancer to never get me but the manifestations in my mind have often been the harder battle. I have wanted to escape my head so many times but eventually, I engaged with services around my PTSD. The analogy of the Bergen army bag was used. When you carry your Bergen you have so much in there, it is a heavyweight but a weight that will save your life. The Bergen would come out and everything in it would be checked, cleaned, checked again and packed away with such precision. My mind was like the Bergen but filled with other people's emotions and burdens and it needed to be emptied, organized and managed. I could not keep storing and carrying others' and my own unhealthy emotions. I am still working on my mental health.

Some days I struggle massively, some days I can just function and other days I almost feel I'm thriving.

I am considered as stable now regarding my cancer and I will have three-month checkups for life. The nerves in my hands and feet are damaged. I am classed as disabled and this impacts me more in the cold months. I take a handful of tablets, which I dislike doing, but I know it is to help me try and function daily. This alone can be hard on my mental health. However, I have a precious four legged helper in my life, my Belgium Shepard therapy dog, Freya.

Last year, I got involved with a charity called Outpost, specifically for veterans. They deliver support for veterans, centred around outdoor pursuits and activities. They have therapy dogs and after attending a session, I was referred to try and access a therapy dog myself. The service, like so many others, was stretched and I was advised it could take a few years. I knew a dog handler in the army and his dog Kuno, was awarded the Dickin medal, for animal service and bravery. I asked him about dogs and their needs and it led me to get Freya. The breed requires a lot of time and for me, it felt like it could help ground me and build up a routine. I am training Freya to achieve her public access qualification before attending therapy dog training programme. She knows how to give cuddles and not to eat off the floor. She stays by my side, watching over me. She is my everything and we have a bond like no other. She loves like your mum but has the bark of a 5 foot PTI if you slack in her exercise. Freya has been the best medicine I could ask for. We are a team, relying on each other. She has saved my life, more than once.

A few years ago, I lost the biggest rock in my life, my nanna. The months leading up to her death, following an initial stroke, were strange. She had held me together my whole life and began telling me important things I had never known. She told me about her father who was in the forces. I had never known about this. He was a medic and was at Dunkirk. Once the anti-aircraft rounds had begun firing, the whistle was blown and the soldiers were told not to proceed. But my great-grandfather refused to stop, seeing people on the beach that still needed assistance. His commander had instructed no more attending to the injured, it was too much of a risk, but he kept driving, seeing someone who needed help. He rescued his brother in arms and received the Military Medal, for gallantry. My nanna had never mentioned this to me, despite being there when I talked about joining the forces all those years ago! Sadly, my nanna passed a few years ago but I am pleased I heard about my great grandfather, a hero.

Freya, my life saver at one of our favourite places, the beach

I learnt a lot in the forces; pride, respect and discipline. Manners learnt from the military and the importance of kindness and compassion. Helping your neighbour and fellow humans. I feel that young people today could benefit from training in the military, rather than learning from the TV. I am grateful for my army time.

When I got involved with Operation Veteran, the director

Jim, told me his inspiring story. He had lost everything, was homeless and an addict. Operation Veteran is safe; I feel safe there and visit when I can. The Wednesday beach walks are magnificent and Freya loves them. It is nice to get out and about, start the day off positively and catch up with the group. They are a great community; welcoming, supportive and kind.

Dedicated to Beano.

Second World War is Declared

Audrey Parsley

Name: Audrey Parsley
Age: 94 years old
Armed Forces, Regiment / Rank: The Women's
Royal Naval Service (WRNS / Wrens), Royal Navy.
Tours / Conflicts served: Germany, 1947.
Date entered: 1946
Date left: 1949

I remember the day that Neville Chamberlain, the then British Prime Minister, declared the start of the Second World War. I was 11 years old and life changed forever. At that moment, I knew I had to become a young adult. At home in Monkseaton, North Tyneside, the air raid sirens began blaring within half an hour. Panic engulfing us, we thought immediately that the Germans were going to land on the beach, not far from our house. Then we discovered it was a test, but the declaration of war was real and for an 11-year-old and my family, it felt that the sound of fear remained in the air for such a long time after that first air raid siren.

My first day at high school was meant to be the following day. Another step in my transition into growing up. I had been eager to experience a new routine, responsibility, learning and friends. It was not to be and instead we were told to wait until we were all prepared for war. This included preparing our family home and the community for an attack. Windows in our homes were reinforced with brown parcel tape, criss-crossed across all window panes as strips of light became darker. Curtains were layered with blackout material attached, to let no sign of life be known to the enemy that may be in the sky, waiting to push death onto us. We placed a bucket of sand and a bucket of water nearby and this method was used until we all had air raid shelters built, in case of an attack.

From that day of the declaration of war, the sense of community and support became as strong as the fear we all held and carried around with us. The heavy cloak of the unknown, of risk and death that we wore wearily. But under-neath that burden lay a heart full of care, compassion and support for our neighbours, friends and family.

The Second World War happened and we got through it. Many from our community, near and far didn't and in those years, life was hard. Growing up was hard. When the war ended in 1946, we all had hope for a better life, a better world.

In 1946 Butlins opened at Filey with the promise of the most wonderful holiday experience, cabaret, plush accommo-dation, food and entertainment. We had finished school and at 18 years old, myself and my friend worked in the council offices at Whitley Bay. We were desperate to visit, our first adventure away from home as adults without the fear and restrictions that war had shackled us with for so many years. A trip was planned and we were like children at Christmas as we got prepared for the holiday of our lives. We planned to share a chalet and met two other girls from London and some boys from London and Gloucester. We all got on swimmingly and had a memorable week, the eight of us together.

Butlins gave me the thrill of adventure I had craved as a young adult. Feeling as free as a bird and enjoying life after feeling oppressed for so long. On my return to the North East from the most wonderful holiday, I couldn't settle down and craved more adventure. I saw an advert for The Women's Royal Naval Service (Wrens) and excitement ran through my mind. Friends and I from school applied for service and I was requested by the navy straight away. I attended a medical in Newcastle, before reporting on 4th December 1946 to Burghfield, Reading, for basic training. Next was a posting to Portsmouth to complete signal training before a journey to Hull's holding camp, as we waited for a ship to take us to Rotterdam. Travelling by ship through the continents at this time felt surreal. We had heard of the destruction from the Second World War, read it in the newspapers and seen it in our own country. Seeing the shores of countries covered in rubble and bomb damage, was like the world had been chewed up and spat out.

We reached the destination of my posting, Hamburg. There had been a full naval party who cleared the rubble and land mines left behind from the war. Our role was to support signals work, and we were there when the Russians closed the borders between the East and West. I was one of ten Wrens altogether to be based in an ex-German officer's house on the banks of the river. It was the most magnificent house, spacious and grand in an area of very little else due to bombing. The bathroom had solid marble features and a bidet, which none of us knew what it was! It was eerie to imagine what had happened there. Hamburg was freezing and we had no fuel to warm the huge house. We managed of course, being the resourceful bunch we were.

Me, in the Wrens (1946)

The Berlin airlift was implemented. The RAF base was right near our accommodation so as the planes took off, they passed our windows every day. They had placed the Short Sunderland patrol bombers to support with the Berlin airlift in the old German Newport base. We would entertain the RAF on an evening with plenty of food and chat. In our accommodation, we had German staff; cooks and a driver. They were lovely people, but the war had left them in poverty and traumatised, they never wanted to talk about it and were grateful for our kindness.

In those days, the Wrens were just like civilians in uniform. Meaning if we went absent without leave, we couldn't get recalled. I was in Germany for around a year and a half, and it was a wonderful experience, meeting people, learning life lessons and playing our part in serving our country.

Dot, myself and 'Chips,' in our Wren Uniforms (1947)

On my return to the UK, I was posted to Admiralty, White-hall, London, near the war offices. I had met my husband-to-be,

Len, whilst out in Germany. I had signed on for three years and this had been completed. I could sign on again with the Wrens if I wished, but after meeting Len, we wanted to get married.

Len was a Royal Marine Commando in the Second World War, joining the forces in 1939. He would refer to D-Day, recalling that he and his comrades were aboard their boats on the 5th of June 1944 and Eisenhower didn't give the call to go to war due to the sea being too rough. He got away before D-Day on the 6th June otherwise he would have been involved with the invasion. He was one of the lucky ones. Len landed in France and travelled to Hamburg, where we met.

We married in December 1949. That is a tale within itself. We were due to get married at St. Peter's Church, Monkseaton. My father, a baker, had made the most stunning three-tiered cake for the day. My father-in-law lived in Dorset and couldn't travel due to ill health, so my own father suggested we all take the wedding to him. On Christmas Day 1949, we set off for Dorset, including our precious cargo, the wedding cake. A local man in Monkseaton had started a taxi business, purchasing a seven-seater American vehicle at the end of the Second World War. My father hired the driver and my parents, my sister and boyfriend, myself and Len travelled down to Dorset, our cake, was neatly protected along with our wedding outfits. Setting off at 6 am on a Sunday morning, we journeyed through all the towns enroute, as there were no motorways in those days. We were able to view all the village nativity scenes on our travels. It was a magical scene of colour and community.

We stopped for lunch at a hotel, hungry and wanting to stretch our legs. At the time, hotels couldn't refuse travellers food, even if it was just a sandwich. We all got ushered to the lounge for a drink before sitting down at 2 pm for a Christmas lunch, a day late. After fuelling ourselves, we set off again and that evening, eventually arrived at my in-law's house in Dorset. My sister was tired so went to bed. Not long after, I joined her, leaving the men to have a few drinks.

The next morning, we were up for the wedding, ready for our ceremony at midday. Adrenaline rushed around my body as I was filled with both nerves and excitement for my special day. However, my sister, Avril was full of cold and my husband-to-be was hungover. They were both unable to enjoy the wedding breakfast, not being able to stomach it for different reasons! In those days, married couples would head straight off on honeymoon after getting married but we tied the knot and returned to my in-laws, for neighbours and family friends to come and wish us well. Len was worse for wear, having drank too much whiskey the night before with my father. He went off to bed, in an attempt to sleep off his hangover. Our driver was also feeling sorry for himself and requested a nap. He ended up in the same bed as my husband, both of them sleeping off too many tipples as I sat downstairs, a few hours into married life!

Luckily, Len had some much-needed sleep to recharge and refresh himself, before returning to his new wife. I had left the honeymoon for Len to sort out, having organised every other aspect of the wedding myself. His mouth fell open, eyes wide as I asked him where he had booked for our magical honeymoon. Stammering, he told me he hadn't booked anywhere! It was a good job I was head over heels in love with him as the first few hours of married life were rather rubbish! Len rang a friend, and we ended up booking a hotel in Swanage, in South East Dorset. Swanage in December had very little to do and felt as cold as I imagined the Arctic to be. We stuck it out for a few nights and despite the cold and limited entertainment, we had a wonderful time. Love was our fuel and anywhere was an adventure with Len.

Len's father had also been in the military, in the Royal Marines, serving on wooden ships. Len himself served for 13.5 years. After we met in Germany, Len returned to the UK and was based at Eastney Barracks, Portsmouth. Once married, we were given a furnished flat down there for a few years. He was a driver and used to drive the director of music for the Portsmouth Royal Marines, Lieutenant-Colonel Sir Francis Vivian Dunn.

My Len, Royal Marine's Army Commando

Len was soon called for deployment to the Malia conflict. He was given a medical, which he failed and was signed out of the military. In those days, companies in civvy street were required to take injured servicemen on as employees. Len completed some mechanics training in Reading and I moved in with my mother-in-law in Dorset during the time. On completion of his mechanical training, he was offered a job in Whitley Bay at Wilson's Garage, so we returned to my hometown. He remained there a while before moving to C.A. Parsons until his untimely death.

Sadly, my Len died in 1972, when he was 52 and I've been a widow for over 50 years. We had two wonderful children together, a boy and a girl. My son was a lighthouse keeper for many years and now is 70 years old, living in Wales with his wife. My daughter is local and a great support. I miss Len every day, we didn't have anywhere near long enough together, but I cherish the love we had in our years of marriage, the memories, the kindness and the companionship.

My father also died when he was young, 50 years old. We had a family business, a bakery that had been passed down from my grandparents. My mother took on the business for a few years before retiring and she was able to support me with childcare when I worked. I spent many years working at the Inland Revenue, which I enjoyed.

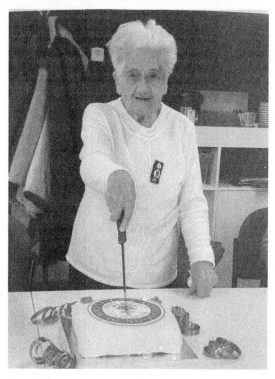

Me (Nov, 2021) at the 75ᵗʰ Anniversary of. W.R.N.S,
Wren Association, North Shields

I try to keep active and as independent as I can, even at 94 years old. I attend many groups including Operation Veteran. I have also been part of a local women's group for over 70 years, three of us being original members. Each Thursday we meet and as time has passed, new women and their adult daughters have joined.

Over the years, I have also been part of conferences, talks, studies and a book about the Wrens. It has been wonderful to share my story. Our group has become smaller as time has gone on, us all reaching old age. It is important to keep the stories alive and I am proud to be part of history.

Dedicated to Len Parsley.

Perfect Palm Reading Prediction
Barbara (Babs) Ann Knowles

Name: Barbara (Babs) Ann Knowles
Age: 78 years old
Armed Forces, Regiment / Rank: Women's Royal Army Corps, Clerical, Lieutenant Corporal
Date entered: 1961
Date left: 1963

I was 17 years old when I joined the Army. Very young but also very focused. I completed basic training at Guildford and then chose my training path in the clerical field which led me to Yeovil. Here I was taught clerical duties such as typing, communications and admin. It was wonderful training and it felt like a perfect role for me. However, I had actually joined the Army for the uniform! I thought it was so smart and professional and was desperate to look the part and also wanted to travel.

After my clerical training, I was posted to the War Office, Landsdowne House in London and I had to wear civilian clothes, after all the dreams of wearing the smart uniform! I could however, wear my uniform on parades and special occasions, but the bubble burst a little, even though the day uniform wasn't too bad. I worked in the WRAC Directorate, the head of the Women's Royal Army Corps in the War Office. One time I was requested to model the new daily uniform, made in a lovat green material, which was to replace the old khaki uniform.

Me, back row, third from right, at Guildford. 1961.

The job was varied and we were trained to be flexible. We were always on standby in case of an emergency or war. Once a year the Princess Royal would come to the War Office for a meeting with the Directorate. Sometime we would be asked to work at the Royal Albert Hall, giving out programmes and welcoming people. Also we would sell programmes at the Royal Variety shows and seeing the stars. Some memorable times that I treasure. I worked at the WRAC Directorate for two years and I loved my job there. I made friends for life, learnt lots of skills and felt part of a team helping the country; one of the many cogs that kept the machine going.

Me, left at Richmond Park Camp (1962)

I met John at the Nuffield Centre in the autumn of 1961, whilst at a dance. John didn't like dancing but he was there with friends, as was I. We all began talking, whilst the music played in the background and the atmosphere thrived. John and I went to the bar and the bartender took both our hands. He turned them over, studying our palms. I glanced at John for a moment, trying not to giggle like a schoolgirl. The bartender looked at us seriously and nodded before telling us that we were going to get married, have three children and we would have a long and happy life together. I smiled, feeling the butterflies of excitement inside my stomach. We had only just met but it was exciting to hear and luckily it didn't scare John off! It turned out, as our lives blossomed, that the bartender was right! All these years later, we are still as in love, have been married for 59 years and have three wonderful children.

On our first planned date, after meeting in the Nuffield Club, we actually stood each other up, both of us unaware at the time. That evening I had attended a Guard's Ball and John had gone ice-skating, neither of us arriving for the planned date. It didn't put us off one another and after meeting again at the Nuffield Club, we became official. John and I got engaged in February 1962, on my birthday and we were married the following year, in March 1963. We decided to get married then as I received a posting to Tripoli, which would mean John and I being separated. Neither of us wanted that and we knew we wanted to marry, so that was settled. However, at this time in the Army, women would be discharged from service once they were married. I had served two years in the forces and marrying John was my priority. After the wedding, I had to report to my barracks in Richmond Park, where I was discharged. We secured our first house in Ealing, London. Home was a lovely flat and our first child, Brenda, was born a year after we married. We remained in London until John was posted to Malaya. John went out ahead of me and I stayed with my parents until accommodation was secured in Malaya.

John and I on our wedding day (March 1963)

Being a military family, posted in different parts of the world, had its ups and downs. On the whole, I would never change our experiences. We had some magnificent postings and I enjoyed all the countries, cultures and the community. Our other two children, Carol and John, were born in Malaya and the three youngsters learnt how to adapt. The children learnt about different people, cultures and experienced travel but it wasn't all plain sailing. At times it could be lonely and I missed my family. We all had to adapt and one of my many skills I developed, was I became an expert at packing up and travelling as light as possible!

To get to Malaya, John's first posting abroad as a family, I travelled on three, eight-hour flights, with a six month old child. On arrival in Singapore, John could not come and meet us, due to the terrorist attacks. Instead, we were escorted in an armed vehicle, weaving through the streets to our hotel. A man sat beside us, machine gun on his lap, ready in case of attack. It was scary. A whole new country, a small child, no husband with me and armed security. It was a shock, even though I had prepared myself somewhat. On our arrival at the hotel, I remember speaking to John on the reception phone and him asking if the hotel had air conditioning. It was stifling hot and our room only had a fan, so climatising was a challenge. Once in our room, I began to unpack and could hear squealing, which turned out to be pigs getting slaughtered nearby! I had been smacked in the face with the new culture I needed to adapt to.

The hotel we stayed at was called the New Seventh Story Hotel. When Singapore underwent a massive modernisation, the hotel survived for many years, even when the majority of buildings across the area were knocked down and rebuilt. I remember John and I returning many years later and seeing the hotel, still standing proud amongst new, modern builds. The lift in the New Seventh Story Hotel had a preservation order on it and the lift itself was just like the ones you see in old films, controlled by an operator. It was eventually demolished, many memories, I am certain were absorbed into the bricks of its structure.

After our first night in Malaya, a humid morning came and we were escorted to the railway station. After travelling to Jahor Bahru, I remember seeing a person on the station platform, and looking twice, realised It was John, with a very deep suntan! It was amazing to be reunited with him and I held him, never wanting to let go. He joined me on the train and after travelling a while, we were told we had to disembark and get onto a bus as the track had been bombed. When we eventually arrived at our accommodation in Bukit Bahru, there was no water. Drinking water was delivered daily to the area. Another challenge to adapt to. We also had to get used to the chit-chat geckos who squatted in our accommodation, crawling in and out as they pleased. They would play hide and seek from us, peeping out from behind pictures on the wall or furniture, before scurrying around, competing in their own lizard races in our home. They were harmless but often gave me a fright.

John enjoyed his job and soon got a role in a small team, overseeing the families medical centre in Bukit Bahru. When John was on night duty, I would get Brenda ready for bed, snuggled in her pram and I would push her the short distance to visit John at work. It was a long night for me without company and it broke up his evening also. I would stay for a while, sometimes just sitting if John had lots to do, observing in admiration of my wonderful husband. He would then watch me walk up the hill, ensuring I got home safely as I pushed the buggy, whilst being alert of the bats circling above me around the street lights.

After our second child Carol was born, John went on tour to Thailand for four months. It was a difficult time for me. I had friends in the wives of other military folk, but I didn't have family to help and we didn't have the sophisticated communication we have today. There were no mobile phones and letters took what felt like an eternity to receive. In these times, it could be isolating, as I waited for John to come home. On one occasion I was waiting for him to come back from Thailand but his flight was cancelled and there was no way of me finding out. That was very frustrating and a worry at the time.

Malaya was my favourite place but John also had postings in Berlin, Cyprus and West Germany, which were lovely. Some difficult but also humorous and amazing times were had in the forces. The good far outweighed the bad. I wouldn't change the life we had and I am very proud of John for his service.

John left the Army in 1981. He was exploring joining the police but at the time there were a lot of disturbances, riots and changes in the police force. However, a BUPA hospital was being built in Norwich where John secured a job, remaining there for almost 20 years. We both joined the Royal Observer Corps in Norwich, staying until it was disbanded in 1990 at the end of the Cold War.

During my time as a forces wife I was lucky enough to secure employment. I worked with the military when we were stationed in Cyprus, with 208 Signals. We were kept busy with work when the Turks invaded Cyprus in 1974. Our next posting was to BMH Rinteln in West Germany where I obtained a job working in the operating theatres preparing the instruments. When the post was filled by military, I went to work as an auxiliary nurse in gynaecology and surgical outpatients department. Eventually, I secured a position completing the admissions and discharges for the hospital until we were posted to Bath in England.

I worked at The Royal National Hospital for Rheumatic

Diseases, Bath, enjoying my time there until we were posted to Norwich, Norfolk. Here, I was successful in getting a job at The Norfolk & Norwich Hospital working in Rheumatology, Oncology and finally in Child Health until retiring in 2004. After six months, the desire to work again led me to securing a bank job working with the NHS & Social Services Learning Disabilities Team. I worked there for seven years, until we moved to Newcastle. This last role was the best and happiest job I ever had, apart from bringing up the family.

Our oldest daughter Brenda, now lives in Australia and works in business travel. Carol, our second daughter, had wanted to join the forces when she was younger. However, she had perforated ears so could not pass the medical and went into banking, now living in Wales. Our son John joined the RAF and served 23 years. He was crew for the AWACS planes and now works as an observer on the police helicopters. We are grandparents and great grandparents and we are very grateful to have such a magnificent family.

John and I, Australia (2019)

In 2011 we relocated to the North East. Our son had been posted at RAF Boulmer and his children were living in Northumberland. Our son needed help for childcare and we wanted to be part of our grandchildren's lives, so we moved up to Northumberland. We were involved in a lot of community groups and had many friends in Norwich, but we still visit and have made friends here. It has been wonderful watching our grandsons grow up, they are phenomenal young men.

John and I play bowls locally, it is a lovely sport and we have made friends and competed in tournaments. We also volunteer once a week at the local hospital and our eldest grandson volunteers alongside us. We visit Operation Veteran and enjoy the service, especially the beach walks. We have made precious friends through the service and it is a community we are honoured to be part of.

I would like to dedicate my small entry of a very small part of my life to my three children Brenda, Carol and John Jnr for coping with the many moves of home, schools and having to leave and make new friends so many times. I love them dearly and thank them for coping with everything over the years.

Forces Family Life

Christopher Wynn

Name: Christopher (Chris) Wynn
Age: 66 years old
Armed Forces, Regiment / Rank: British Army –
RAMC (Royal Army Medical Corps), Captain
Date entered: Feb 1987
Date left: Feb 1995

I joined the Territorial Army (TA) in 1983 as a test, to assess if I enjoyed it. I was interested in the army and knew if I enjoyed the TA, I would likely be happy and do well in the regular army. The TA was great and I attended an interview for the regular army in November 1986 to join the RAMC (Royal Army Medical Corps). It was a rush as I started in February 1987, but I didn't find out until December 1986. There was a lot to organise and my wife, Denise was pregnant at the time, expecting our third child. Our sons, Russell and Christopher were very young, Christopher only being a baby.

My wife stayed at home whilst I completed basic training for almost six months; comprising of a six-week course at

Sandhurst, then further training at the RAMC training
centre, Keogh Barracks, Aldershot. My first posting was at
Aldershot, where I spent just under two years working as a
medic. In June 1987, my wife, Denise and our two sons
joined me at Aldershot. We were given our first quarters, a
four bedroomed house next to the barracks. Soon after, our
third child Lara, was born in Cambridge Military Hospital. I
remember when Denise went into labour I told the medical
team that it was my birthday. I was desperate for our daughter
to be born on the same day as her dad. Time wasn't on our
side, then at last, Lara was born five minutes to midnight, on
my birthday!

Sandhurst (1987). Me: Third row, sixth from left

My next posting after Aldershot was a 12-month stint in
Rinteln, Germany. It was a great posting and I enjoyed my
work there. The children and Denise settled well and for me,
it was lovely having my family with me. We made great
memories, even the ones that caused us anxiety, like the night
we couldn't find our youngest son, Christopher. That specific
night our front door was open and Christopher was nowhere
to be seen. Panic rose in us, Christopher wasn't even four

years old. I began shouting his name, anxiety engulfing me as I made my way away from our front door. My heart racing, I heard Denise shout my name from the house. She had found our son, sleeping on the large windowsill, behind the thick curtains, blissfully unaware of the sheer panic inflicted on us. We lost him again not long after in a shop. Everyone in the shop got involved, trying to find him and he was hiding in the middle of a large rack of clothes, giggling away as the adults flustered in the commotion. We have some great memories of our children during my time in the army and often recite them, much of the time to embarrass our children who are now in their 30s and 40s, it's our parental duty!

After Germany, we were posted back to Woolwich for two and a half years. During this time, I took part-time work at Kings College hospital, with the transplant team to supplement my work in the RAMC. Often, I would support the team at Kings College to collect livers for transplants, travelling the country.

Me, in Aldershot (1988)

During our time in Woolwich, I was sent out on detachment to The Falklands Islands. It was the middle of October 1991, just at the start of the first Gulf War. I always say it was the posting that was never meant to happen. It was the first time I had been away from Denise for any length of time, so it was going to be hard from the beginning, for us all. Denise had driven me to the station at Woolwich, where I would get my train to RAF Brize Norton. She was very tearful, knowing it was my job but also carrying the worry of all military spouses like an albatross around the neck. I was reluctant to leave, but knew I had to. It was my job and my duty. I embraced my wife, telling her time would speed past and I would be back home in soon, not realising it really would be a short time!

Off I went on the train, leaving my wife and young children behind with a heavy heart. I arrived at Brize Norton and there was only one plane available to the Falklands. I was informed that there was a problem with the plane, resulting in a flight delay of 36 hours. Eventually, we took off but there was something wrong, I felt it immediately. The pilot calmly announced we were returning to base to inspect the plane. On arrival back to Brize Norton, it transpired that there had been an accident. There was a road that ran across the flight runway, operated by traffic lights. The lights had been on green and a Land Rover was travelling across the path of the plane taking off. The plane and Land Rover collided, taking the roof of the vehicle off. It was extremely lucky that no one was killed and the realisation of the very near miss shook me.

After that debacle, we eventually flew out to Ascension Island and then onto the Falkland Islands. Once we landed, I was excited about the posting and spent the first four weeks happily conducting my job as a medic. I'll always remember one time when we had a call, a road traffic accident, where a local had crashed his motorcycle. There was extensive damage, including to his liver, which was ruptured. The surgeon on duty was orthopaedic, so not necessarily experienced with this type of injury. After consideration, there were two surgical options and we picked one as a team. Luckily, the patient survived and after a few weeks in hospital, went on his merry way. He was very grateful and thanked us all, sincerity in his eyes. It was a wonderful feeling, we saved a man's life and I loved that part of my job. It never left me and I was lucky enough to continue practicing medicine after my army days. My daughter also went into nursing, psychiatric nursing. Medicine, health care and supporting people in need have always been something we have been able to share.

One day in the Falklands, it was quiet and some of us decided to go for a 20-mile walk around the three hills of Stanley. I turned up, eager to go, with my training shoes on. One of the crew advised me I would need my boots as it was quite an arduous terrain. I nodded and headed back for my boots, excitement and the need to not delay the group being my fuel. A minute later I was down on the ground after hitting a loose rock, stumbling and breaking my ankle in the process. I lay there, pain searing through my ankle, knowing all too well it was game over. My colleagues still went on the walk as I went to the hospital. I had to undergo surgery to repair my ligaments. It meant I was out of action, like a bicycle with a puncture and ordered to return home, in time for Christmas, much to Denise's delight.

This also meant I had to be posted in a base camp and therefore I didn't get sent out to the then, war zone. Denise was understandably relieved and I could still do much of my job whilst getting physio on my ankle.

When I arrived home, Denise didn't inform the children. Instead, she took them into the Queen Elizabeth military hospital, where I was getting treated and ready for discharge. She told the children they were going for their haircut and they happily went along with the story. On arrival, I was there waiting. It was a wonderful surprise and their faces shone brighter than the sun. We can still see it now, even 30 years later.

Me: Coming out of the hospital in the Falklands; the posting that was never meant to be.

Throughout my time in the forces, I saw some difficult cases. I was working at Cambridge military hospital, there was a memorable patient. Ireland was still experiencing conflict and we had a patient, only 18 years old who was less than two months out of his basic training. He was sent to Northern Island and hit by an anti-personnel mine across his body, which blew off his lower legs and manhood. He survived, but I often think about it and how that young man coped as an adult, with such a life altering injury. We did our best, in all cases to save people, treat them and assist them in recovery. It was our job. It was more than a job, it was my calling, my passion. But it was still challenging at times and some cases will always stay with me. Despite the passing of time, they linger like old ghosts.

My next posting was Hong Kong, a posting I had requested and was pleased to receive. We spent two years there as a family of five, which was a magnificent experience and great for our children's education and socialisation. As with any new culture, it took us time to adapt. I remember when we arrived, getting off the plane, we were hit with a blast of warmth. Denise looked at me, eyes wide and said she hoped the heat was from the plane engines. It wasn't! It was stifling and it took us a long time to adjust. I loathe shopping, but in Hong Kong, I loved shopping. I spent a lot of my non-working time in Hong Kong in the shopping malls; they were one of the only cool places with air-con. I became an avid shop browser! A distressing incident happened to us as a family whilst we were in Hong Kong. All of our belongings, left in storage at home, were destroyed in a fire. Sentimental items from our childhood and lives to date, including photos of our wedding and family, items passed to us, as well as expensive bits of furniture, all ruined. We were devastated. Everything was gone. Six months later, we received a parcel in the post. We had unknowingly left a photo album in our old house in one of the sideboards and the new owners had sent it to us. It was priceless and we felt like we had won the lottery when we received it, crying and clasping it. To this day we are grateful to the people who sent it. We also managed to get copies of our wedding photos, thanks to family members. Furniture was gone however, so when we returned to the UK, we brought some beautiful furniture from Hong Kong, including tables, lamps and magazine racks, which we still have a few pieces of today.

Whilst in Hong Kong, Denise got a job as a Teaching Assistant. She loved it and spent a lot of time one-to-one with the children, who were aged seven to eight. It was nice for Denise to have her own identity, work and meet people whilst I worked in the army. We also had an Amah (maid) in Hong Kong, who was lovely. It was strange for us culturally and she had previously been treated appallingly. She loved working with us and became part of the family.

For the children, the door to experiences they would never have the opportunity to try, opened. They flourished, but family life in the army wasn't without its challenges. Christopher was starting a new school in Hong Kong and we went for a visit. He looked at me, biting his lip before the Headteacher spoke. I saw my son breathe a sigh of relief, his shoulders dropping as a smile crept onto his face. He told me later that he thought he was going to have to speak Chinese, not realising it was an English-speaking school. He had been ruminating, worrying about not being able to communicate with anyone. The army taught the children confidence, different lifestyles and cultures.

During our time in Hong Kong, we visited Australia with our army air miles. It was another amazing adventure for us and the children. We visited Newcastle, our hometown's namesake. It was a much longer train journey than we thought on the map but coming out of the train station, we saw buses to Wallsend via Jesmond. It was magical seeing our home town on the opposite side of the world.

Denise and me at Newcastle, Australia

Although we loved Hong Kong, it was difficult to manage everyday life in ways. It was such a busy city, even then, jam-packed with people everywhere. It was claustrophobic and overwhelming at times. When our almost two years in Hong Kong came to an end, we were ready for a change in many ways.

On return from Hong Kong, I was posted to Woolwich, then returned to Catterick for my final posting of my eight-year service. Once my army medic days were finished, I knew I wanted to continue my career in nursing. I left the army, returning to civvy street and I found a job in Barnsley, as a charge Nurse. We all planned to move, the removal van was full and even included Denise's mini cooper car, to save us driving two cars to our new home. Then the house sale fell through last minute. As a family, we ended up living in a hotel for a short period before we found a rental property. We eventually bought a house and settled.

Part of the readjustment to civvy street was hard. The upheaval of finding a new job and a new home, was challenging with a young family. We also missed the social side of the military. There were so many events, dances, meals and social opportunities in the Mess.

All of our lives changed when I left the military, but our time as a family in the army continued to impact. One time, our eldest son, Russell was on-line. He began chatting to a girl, Tina Louise, about his time in the army, in particular Woolwich. It transpired that Tina Louise lived very close to where we had lived in our quarters. Russell and Tina Louise communicated for some time before meeting up in the Midlands. They soon fell in love and married. This was 17 years ago and we have a wonderful grandson. A magical legacy from our time in the forces.

I spent the rest of my working career in the medical field,

settling back in the North East after a period in Barnsley. I retired when I was 60 years old as an elective orthopedic team manager. We now have our retirement apartment, with its own community and activities. It's safe, secure, homely and we have all we need as we get older. We go to Operation Veteran and have friends there and of course, our wonderful family. Life is good.

We made friends for life in the military who we still keep in touch with and visit. Friendships are made in camaraderie that will last forever, no matter the distance, no matter the years that pass. Those people who will always understand; the horror of conflict, the foundations of teamwork that life or death was built on. They know the family that the armed forces become, the friendships forged that will stand the test of the longest time.

Dedicated to all the service people who we have lost.

Boys Become Men
Dave Watson

Name: Dave Watson
Age: 74 years old
Armed Forces, Regiment / Rank: Royal Navy:
Leading Radio Operator. British Army: Commando Gunners
Conflicts / Tours served: Indonesian Conflict (1965)
Date entered: 1964
Date left: 1975

My uncle served in the Royal Navy, a Leading Stoker in the
Royal Signals. He was conscripted during the Second World
War but was killed by a torpedo. I never got to meet him, but
his story and bravery planted a seed of desire in me to join the
navy.

I started life after school as an apprentice plumber,
following in my father's footsteps. One night I was making my
packed lunch for the following day and I had a lightbulb
moment. I realised if I didn't leave my apprenticeship, I would
likely spend my life as a plumber, something I simply didn't
want to do. The next day, I visited the Royal Navy recruit-

ment centre and at 16 years old, I was just a boy. The navy recruitment team gave me a book of information to take away and digest, but I had already made my mind up. I wanted in! I just had to convince my parents to sign the form, since I was under 18 years old.

My father seemed secretly pleased that his son wanted to go into the big, wide world and protect his country. My mother on the other hand, was less comfortable with the thought. Her brother had died in conflict and at 16, I was still really her baby son. I waited patiently, in hope that my parents would agree for me to join. The days dragged and I couldn't sleep with the excitement of what the future could hold for me. A week later, after much chatting and I am certain much convincing from my father to my mother, the forms were signed. They were handed to me by my parents with the realisation that their strong minded son had made a decision and three weeks after my 16th birthday, I was signed up with the Royal Navy.

I left home, the eagerness for exploration bursting through my veins. Basic training of six weeks commenced at HMS Raleigh and then I was sent to HMS Mercury for training at Signal School. I finished my training and completed my preference form, indicating which part of the world I would like to be stationed in. Rosyth, Scotland had been my choice. I was dating a girl back home in Newcastle and thought it would be close enough to maintain the relationship. The Royal Navy sent me to Singapore! The romance fizzled as I travelled across the other side of the world, but to me, the thought of adventure was my new love.

Me at HMS Raleigh (May, 1964)

In Singapore, I was stationed at the Naval base, HMS Terror and I was part of the fleet pool, meaning I would go where needed. I quickly ended up on a minesweeper. As a young lad, I didn't take much notice of the politics of the world. Of course, I understood war and serving the country, that's why I joined the navy. Well that and to experience life, travel, and grow as a person. I had little understanding and interest in politics. At the time, President Sukarno of Indonesia aimed to conquer Malia, Singapore, Borneo and Brunei and Sarawak, as well as other countries. Troops and agent provocateurs were sent by sea to cause unrest. The boat I was on at the time was part of a patrol to monitor Sukarno's direction.

On my first night on board the ship, we were standing there, myself alongside another newly trained rating. we heard a ferocious bang, bang, bang. Many of the crew hit the deck, like dominos falling on a table. Myself and my shipmate remained standing, wondering what was going on. The high-velocity rounds continued. All of a sudden, one went to the right of my shipmate, one in the middle of us and another to the left of us. We looked at each other, silent, our mouths open. It was then that the penny dropped and we also dived on the deck, absorbing the realism that we were the target of attack.

The battle went on for 90 minutes. I found out when we sailed back into Singapore the following day, the result of those 90 minutes of conflict; 19 of the enemy were captured and multiple casualties occurred. Up until then, ignorance had been bliss. The motivator in my young mind had been that war was a big adventure, the boy zone! Whilst it could still be an adventure, it became so much more and my brain switched. It converted to focus on protecting, serving and managing the crisis. I was a 16-year-old boy that become a man, well almost.

Following this attack, I was told by my superior that my action station during the hours of darkness would be on top of the bridge. Here I would be watching for the enemy approaching, with illumination rounds from a two-inch mortar. The locals still took the risk of fishing at night, desperate to keep their livelihood. As soon as any movement was picked up, the contact station would alert us. Then we would go to our action stations, ready and waiting like an eagle preying on a mouse. Any boats identified would be challenged and ordered to stop, if they didn't the illumination rounds would be fired. All the teams had various weapons and knew how and when to discharge them, after all, we were in plain sight of the enemy. Vigilance was paramount, it was life or death. Where we had a grandstand view of the enemy, they equally had the same view of us. We were all vulnerable and quick action was survival.

At such a young age, it was hard to comprehend. I felt

immortal. Bad things happen to other people, not you. That's what we always think, surely everyone is guilty of that in life? But when you are out there, looking death in the eye, telling it you aren't ready yet, fighting for survival for you and your comrades. Well in those life-changing moments, boys become men.

Whilst away with the forces, I would write to my mother at home in North Tyneside. Nowhere near as frequently as I should have. Selfishly and ironically, given my job in the navy was communications, I hardly thought of home, my parents and my sister. As a parent myself, it's hard to even begin to comprehend how worried my mother and father must have been. I now appreciate the suffocating anxiety a parent feels to protect their child. But back then, well I was too busy doing my duty and perhaps, somewhere, a little part of me didn't want my parents to worry. Or maybe part of me didn't want to document some of the scary reality of conflict.

In my earlier days of serving, I made the mistake of writing to my mother after receiving correspondence from her. She had written that she and my father had seen two ships on the news that they had been involved in a large battle. She had commented that she was, "Glad I hadn't been on it." Of course, I had been on the ship and replied to her letter telling her just that, in a blasé manner as if to say I would have a cup of coffee rather than tea. Needless to say, my mother didn't appreciate it and I realised some things were best not to mention, at least until the conflict was over.

I wrote less and less as time went on. In desperation, my mother went to the extreme of writing to me with, "If alive reply. If dead, don't bother." She was clearly trying other tactics to get her son to communicate. Thinking I was clever, I smugly wrote back with one word only, "Missing." I did however write a slightly longer letter to my father, I wasn't that cruel.

A few years later, in 1968, there was an incident that I still think about. I had worked with an army unit in Singapore for a week and loved it. Thinking it was the life for me, I enquired about getting into the unit and one of the criteria was to pass an all arms commando course. One of the sections for this was ploughing through a water tunnel; basically travelling across a stream that had been dammed, where a narrow makeshift tunnel had been created. The task had to be completed as a team, passing weapons and pulling and pushing each other through the tunnel. During the exercise, I got trapped and almost drowned. Feeling the world close in on me as I struggled to get free. After what felt like an eternity, I managed to get out. Shaking and pale, I looked at the officer, who simply asked if I was going to do it again.

"Yes Sir," I announced, mustering as much courage as I could, despite my legs feeling like jelly. I was fully aware that if I didn't try again, I wouldn't pass the course. Smothering the fear, I managed to get through the tunnel a second time round and wrote to my mother telling her I nearly drowned. About a week later, I got a message telling me I had to go to see the commanding officer at the training wing.

"Watson, I've had a letter from your mother. She wants you off the course as it's too dangerous." He bellowed at me, his stern eyes not blinking.

I was mortified. I wanted to shuffle away in shame. I knew I had a split second to reverse the embarrassment and the commanding officer's likely view that I was incapable. Instead, I cleared my throat and confidently said, "Only two things will get me off this course Sir; you and your staff because you don't think I am good enough or myself because I have given up. I won't be giving up Sir and I will be having a word with my mother the next time I get home." I stood tall and he looked at me, nodded and replied abruptly with, "Right, march out."

That was it settled and another lesson learnt; to not tell my mother what was happening. For the rest of my time in the military, I didn't disclose any near-death experiences, keeping letters generic and as positive as was realistic.

After the commando course, the parachute course was a further test. I passed and during my next period of home leave, I jokingly gave my wings badge to my father. During the Second World War, my father and his friend got bored learning morse code. They had desired another challenge and so volunteered for a new airborne brigade. My father and his friend were sent to Ringway airport in Manchester for training. When they realised the depth of what was involved, they quickly decided to return to the boredom of the Royal Signals. It gave me great pleasure to hand over my wings to him for the ones he never got!

In reality, I understood my father and his friends' reservations. On the parachute course, we had to do two jumps from the old-fashioned barrage balloon and six from an aircraft. On one of the jumps, I saw another canopy above me. It was another parachutist and he was walking across my canopy. It was very dangerous and during my time in the forces, I lost count of the number of near misses. Luck was on my side on more occasions than I could have imagined.

I joined 148 Battery with the Commando Gunners after these courses. I travelled to Scotland to learn to ski in preparation for a winter warfare course in Norway. I was posted in various countries; Norway, Singapore, Malta and Libya.

In Libya, when the troops were on the move again, some of us stayed on for an extra week. One night we walked throughout the night to reach another camp. It was the desert but quite flat and we were all fit lads, deciding it would be a challenge easy to conquer. On our travels, we were picking up empty cartridge cases from .303 Lee Enfield rifles and found old, rusty jerry cans, both artefacts from the Second World War. As we trekked, we would look up into the dark sky and see flashes of light on the horizon, followed by banging. At the time British troops used Libya as a training location. I'll never forget how surreal it felt; history in front of us, on the ground and in our hands, yet the reality of conflict in the present. Behaviours repeating themselves over two decades later.

We eventually reached our destination camp and were welcomed in. The soldiers were dumfounded as to how we had managed to walk overnight across the desert to get there, wondering where our vehicle was.

During my time in the navy and army, I learnt so much. I was a sponge, soaking up the knowledge, experiences and views of the world. It was the greatest lesson I could have asked for as a youngster. Lessons that shaped me as a person, gave me the foundation to go on and be the adult, husband, father and grandfather I am. It was a lesson in life and humanity and I learnt about obsessions, the extremes people go to in their ideology – the instigator of so many conflicts. I was educated in politics and influence, opinions, values and beliefs. I learnt that difference can be a wonderful thing or a wicked thing.

In Singapore, President Sukarno wanted more land for his people. Greed pushed his influence onto his countries soldiers and ultimately, it failed. Sukarno never got more land and instead, hundreds of people were killed, the majority of fatalities being his people.

The whole conflict woke me up to how things could be in the world and that the world was much bigger and at times, far worse than the small town in North East England where I spent my first 16 years of life. People will always have different opinions, the two sides to a coin.

Everywhere I worked in the forces, especially like the Commando's, there was a 'can do,' attitude. We worked in a team of five, led by an officer. We became more than colleagues, we became family. It was 24/7 with each other; the good, the bad and the ugly. It's what gets you through, but most importantly gets your team through. In times when we could have all died, we had a solution, a collective answer. We had each other's back and even if people didn't click as friends or personalities clashed, in the moment of need; in the field, at sea, in the air, we had each other's back. Solidarity. Respect. Loyalty.

Alongside the horror and depravity of the enemy, we also came across the kindness of humanity. One time during winter warfare in Norway, we went exploring for coffee. On our travels, skiing down the track, a woman flagged us down. She invited us into her home for food. It was such a treat for us and we gratefully accepted. The family had a four-year-old son, who was fascinated by our uniforms and badges. He looked shyly but with great curiosity. I put my boots and skis back on and returned up the track to our camp where I proceeded to go into others' tents and cut some of my fellow soldiers' badges off their uniforms. Military parachute wings were taken, the Artillery cap badge and others. I returned to the Norwegian family with my bounty and handed them to the boy. His face illuminated with the biggest smile as he held his treasure in his little palm. It was a priceless moment, for us all and we had a lovely night with our new friends.

Another time in 1967, we were in Greece and visited a bar. It was full of locals as we walked in, dressed in our British Army uniforms. We looked above the bar and there was a huge picture of Sir Winston Churchill, wearing his trademark

Homberg hat and a cigar hanging out of her recognisable mouth. The bar owner refused to let us pay all night and with humble gratitude told us time and time again that they could not thank us enough for what the Royal Navy did for the Greek people during the Second World War. It was an emotional night for everyone and one I won't ever forget.

Me, Bangkok, Thailand (Feb, 1975)

Kindness continued after I left the forces. One time, my wife, Pauline and I took our granddaughter swimming at the local baths. My wife got talking to a Malay couple, mentioning I served in Asia and that I could speak a little Malay. The next time we were at the swimming baths, we saw the couple again. They gifted me a little statue of the Petronas Towers in Kuala Lumpur and some local currency. The man proudly handed me the gift, clasped my forearm and told me it was a small thank you for what we had done to help their country all those years ago in the 1960s. Decades had passed, but gratitude remained. Kindness was never forgotten.

I left the forces in 1975, aged 27. On reflection, it was short-sighted and a little stubborn of me. I had thought about leaving then changed my mind, but by this point, to remain I would have had to go through my training again. I spat my dummy out and left.

For a few years after leaving the forces, I did very little. I struggled with purpose, dossing about here and there. Looking back, it was clear adjusting to life outside of the navy and army was a challenge. The forces had been my whole adult experience to date and I knew very little else of civilian adult life. My routine, my daily life, my discipline, my purpose; the navy and army had created it all. I didn't know who I was outside of the military and it felt like my identity was in the wind, travelling away from me.

I would get up most days and go to the pub, come back, go for a run then back to the pub. A mental and physical struggle of lack of purpose but wanting to keep the discipline of exercise. A monotonous cycle on repeat. I felt lost. Some days, to break up the soul-destroying pattern, I would go parachuting at Sunderland airport. One day I had my awakening, the catalyst I had needed for far too long, to change my life.

I had been to Sunderland drinking and I had returned to the airport to sleep there, ready to fly on a Sunday. I had drunk a lot of alcohol, you had to be drunk to sleep in the bunk house. It was filthy and the bed bugs would pull the blanket up for you! Sunday morning, I was sitting in the clubhouse drinking orange juice and one of the lads smiled at me and said, "That wasn't a bad jump this morning was it?"

I looked at him, rubbing my forehead. My heart started racing. It transpired, three of us had gone up to 5000 feet and jumped free fall that morning. I couldn't recall any of it due to my still drunken state from the night before. It got me. My wake-up call picked me up there and then, shaking me violently. The realisation that my luck would run out and I wasn't immortal. Life had to change and it did.

At the time, I hadn't long been courting my now wife, Pauline. She helped pull me back to reality and gave me a reason to focus on my future. She was a wonderful, stabilising influence on my life. I soon found regular work and Pauline and I married. After 10 or so years, I got a job working for the police, as a civilian. I stayed in the police until I retired. A few years later my teacher daughter, Angela, asked if I wanted to work as an exam invigilator. I said yes and I still do it now. I have hobbies which include riding my motorbike and attending the groups at Operation Veteran, where Pauline comes along too.

Pauline and me, Queen Elizabeth II memorial service (September, 2022)

I remain married to my darling Pauline. I'm not perfect, I can be selfish at times, I'm human after all. But we have been good for each other and love one another dearly. We are a great team and we have a lovely family. I've had health scares and I appreciate life. The navy and army began teaching me that important lesson, all those years ago.

Dedicated to those who never came back. They are the real heroes.

From Covert to Councilor

Gary Bell

Name: Gary Bell

Age: 59 years old

Armed Forces, Regiment / Rank: Royal Air Force, Special Communications, Junior Technician

Conflicts / Tours served: Belize, Various Locations UK, Holland

Date entered: 1979

Date left: 1993

I left school in 1979, aged 16 years old. There were few prospects where I lived in North Tyneside. The coal mining pits, which had been a major industry, were closing. My dad worked at the shipyards, another local industry, but had previously been a Royal Engineer whilst completing his National Service. I loved sport, especially rugby and cricket at school. It was a massive part of my life and my dream was to incorporate it into any job that I could. This was where the RAF came in. RAF Cosford had a running track and full sports facilities. It became of great interest to me. Another magnetic pull to the RAF came when I visited the recruiting office in Newcastle. I looked on the map of where I would train, studying the location of the bases. They were close to train stations and I thought I could incorporate my love for Newcastle United, with away games. The decision was made and I signed up to join the RAF.

I completed basic training at RAF Swinderby, before spending a year, completing my trade training at RAF Cosford. The training was difficult, understandably, but I was still able to indulge in my passion for playing rugby, forming part of a team there. I never wanted to join to kill the enemy and was not very much into the Royal Family and although I immersed myself in the military way of life and my training, the trade and sports were the appeal to me. We didn't have to conduct guard duty and polish our shoes very often once we finished trade training. Instead, I felt like I got the golden ticket that meant I had a career and a trade but also my favourite hobby.

Our home base was around a mile away from the rest of the camp and limited people were allowed access, to ensure intelligence safety and security. My training and role were very specialised and once training was complete, I worked with a team across Europe, working out of GCHQ (Government Communication Headquarters). Initially, I was posted to RAF Buchan, Peterhead. It wasn't the best site, but I met my wife Linda there when I was 18 years old, two days after arriving. It felt like fate, she made such an impression on me and we've been together since. Linda and I married in February 1983 and had a transient life, moving seven times in ten years. We took it in our stride, both being able to adapt and grateful we had one another. I often think that it must have been difficult for Linda at times, me not being a regular husband and my role being so specialist. All Military wives deserve a medal, they are amazing. I owe so much to Linda. Despite our love for one another, we did have challenges, one being whilst serving at Raf Saxa Vord, in the Shetlands. During this time, Linda had a miscarriage which was a very sad time for us. We were, however, blessed with Louise born 1986 at Inverness, Lindsey 1990 at Lincoln.

Security clearance was of the highest level due to the work I was involved with. The job was very much like a civilian role and I worked four days on and four days off, allowing me time for rugby. Our remit was to identify Russian air crafts 5-6,000 miles away by electronic signatures. From day one, it was forbidden to discuss anything with anyone outside of the team, including your family. We learnt this in our training and the importance of the consequences of a security breach. At times there were things on the news that we knew about as they had already happened, but we were unable to breathe a word, signing up to carry our knowledge to the death. Intelligence could easily get into the wrong hands and have catastrophic consequences. When Gorbachev was deposed in the Black Sea, in 1991, ending the coup which saw him under house arrest, we knew before it was announced to the world.

Linda and I on our wedding day (Feb 1983)

Our team would monitor the movements of many Russian large aircrafts. Our concern would be around the movement of nuclear weapons and sharing intelligence with our armed forces. We were a small team of five per shift and on detachments there was always someone you knew. This was good in some respects; knowing each other's skills and how they worked. It wasn't as great if you clashed with someone and ended up stuck working closely with them for a long period of time.

I had a two-year posting in Holland in 1986 -1988. We lived in a lovely place, Maastricht. Linda and our six-month-old daughter, Louise, joined me. We had a nice home and I worked locally. Linda, Louise and I lived in a flat with our Dutch neighbours. I worked on the border between Holland and Belgium so at work, I would be in Belgium but return home to Holland. The base was deep inside a cave. Getting to the actual office wasn't great but once inside, you would never think it was inside a cave, the main reason why it was located there! We had everything we needed, equipment and resources.

On the night shift, half of us would stay awake and half of us would sleep or go to the bar on site, inside the caves! It was called the Mushroom Bar and we would drink the local Belgium beer before having a nap. There was a vending machine in the cave. This wasn't your usual vending machine with hot chocolate and coffee or crisps and biscuits. It sold beer. When money was tighter, usually before payday, we would compete with the Americans, who were also based in the cave with us to get on shift first, empty the beer from the vending machine and charge the losing nation extra to buy it from us. It was a brilliant posting, not just for the beer!

We did do actual work in Belgium and at the time. Much of it was for NATO. Some of the crew were conscripts and had minor roles like cleaning and maintenance. Some sections of the unit, like where we were based, were for more sensitive information. It was monitoring in case of a further war, being on standby.

After this posting, we returned to the UK and I was posted to a base RAF Pitreavie Castle, Edinburgh. There were limited places we could be posted in special comms and at this unit, I was told I would be working at a specialist unit located nearby. On my arrival, it transpired I would be working with the Royal Navy in an underground facility. Whilst serving the terrorist act at Lockerbie took place the evening I was on duty and I was also on duty when the tragedy of the Piper Alpha explosion occurred in the North Sea.

Another good role was when I served at RAF Kinloss. I would leave home, go to unit and collect sensitive information. It would be stored in a locked briefcase, chained around my wrist. I would be driven to Inverness airport and put on the plane, usually the first customer. We would arrive in London and I would be the last off the plane. I would then be collected by a driver and taken to Bushy Park where the briefcase would be handed over and the sensitive information taken. Then I would return to Inverness but usually have some time in London first, visiting museums and tourist sites.

During my career, I also spent time at Raf Digby or Raf North Luffenham. In the RAF, I sustained an injury and lost the use of my left arm. I had to go to the RAF Hospital and received electric shock treatment in my neck for my nerves. I never regained full strength in my left-hand side. I still played rugby, but it wasn't the same. Leaving the RAF, the hardest part was leaving the rugby. There was a defence review in 1993 and we were told there would be no promotions for three years. I was due for a promotion and it pushed me to sign off and leave the RAF. The rugby season was due to start again in September, I timed my departure so I could finish the season of my beloved sport. It was a big loss in my life, but it was the right time for me to leave the RAF.

There were some frustrating times working in special comms. The level of analysis of your every move and security clearance could feel like you were constantly being watched.

Privacy was invaded and every part of your life was investigated, dissected, and questioned. I understood the critical nature of the role and the need for this, but so many times it felt suffocating. Each year, I would be interrogated by the RAF police. They would ask about my relationships and they would access my bank accounts. All statements would be analysed in case I was getting blackmailed or paid for information. Every transaction would be queried and any anomalies scrutinised.

In 1985, I was at home and there was an event for the miners. Being a socialist and caring about local industry, I attended. They were raising money, so I wrote a cheque for the cause. When I was questioned by the RAF police, they asked if I was a communist. They queried why I was contributing to the miner's welfare and I had to explain I came from a mining community. My family history would be investigated, including Linda's family. People would be watched now and then in the pubs they drank in case any information was shared unintentionally as alcohol loosened the lips.

There was a special unit in the RAF hospital for people in my trade as it was renowned for taking people to breaking point. My job was one of the less intense ones, but some roles in special comms must have felt like they carried the world on their shoulders and lived a complete double life, both of which would have felt very isolating. We referred to 'the cabbage patch,' which was an area where people had to type morse code constantly at a pressurised speed. Many of the workers in this unit had mental health breakdowns.

In 1993, an option when leaving special comms was to go and work for the GCHQ. At the time, I was married to Linda and our daughters, Louise and Lindsey were young. We didn't want to keep moving our family around as the girls were of school age. We came home to the North East and I knew I would struggle to get work, given how niche my skill set was. When I left the RAF, my passport was marked and I was unable to travel to places such as Cuba for ten years in case I leaked any information. It was strange readjusting to the fact that I could talk about life a lot more freely, just not my life in the RAF.

I found the transition back to Civilian very hard and nearly re-joined the RAF. I was offered a role with the defence establishment, basically guarding military sites. I then saw a job in the local paper for an office manager with Northumbria Police. I applied and was successful in getting the role. After a year applied for a role within the communications team, I worked on the phones, dispatching units and working with the gold command, events such as football matches and VIP visits. I worked there until 2011 and I also had the honour of being a Unison shop steward, helping staff with appeals against dismissal. It was a great job but in 2011 there was a meeting about redundancies. At the time, in 2011 I was in my late 40s and I took redundancy.

In 2012 I secured a job at Tesco Insurance and in May of the same year, I stood for election in my local borough and was elected. My mam was a trade unionist and I had always been part of the union. I've been a socialist all my life so standing for local government and supporting the borough I grew up in, felt like a natural step for me. Unfortunately, it meant I couldn't stay at Tesco, due to my council commitments, so I left. A few other jobs followed, including a short stint working with my daughter and a job at PayPal. I never settled though and nothing felt the right fit.

In 2013, Norma Redfearn became Elected Mayor and she asked me if I would like to be North Tyneside Council's Armed Forces Champion, to raise the profile in the commu-

nity. I was delighted and embarked on the challenge. Through
our work at North Tyneside Council, we made big steps to

support our armed forces
community and influenced
change through policies and
practice. I would visit organisations asking them what they
needed and familiarise myself
with what we were offering, or
not offering in the area for veterans. In 2015, I became chair of

*Me, left at The Somme (1ˢᵗ
July, 2016)*

the council, which was another honour. I began meeting more
people and strengthening our offer in North Tyneside to
veterans and their families. In 2017, we were awarded the
Gold Covenant Award, the highest award available.

*Me at Freedom of the Borough,
Tynemouth Voluntary Life
Brigade (2015)*

In 2013, I decided it would
be wonderful to run a breakfast
club for veterans in the area. I
had noticed there was a gap in
provision and felt it could bring
people together for companionship and support. We applied to
the Armed Forces Covenant and
they awarded us £10,000. The
breakfast club mobilised, starting off in Wallsend on a
Tuesday afternoon. Jim, from Operation Veteran began
attending it.

Then life changed once again when Colin Back from
Project Nova, an early intervention project for veterans in the
criminal justice system, contacted me. They offered support
to veteran offenders, victims, or both. The service was
running in other police force areas and they were interested in
duplicating the service in the North East. I connected Project

Nova to our police force and our Police and Crime Commissioner at the time supported the scheme to run. Project Nova then asked if I would do the role, working with the police and supporting veterans who may benefit from the service. I thought the role might only last a year or two, I am still there seven years later! It is a brilliant service that supports veterans in need and connects them with other services, such as Operation Veteran.

Me, Chair of the Council (May, 2015)

After starting at Project Nova, I asked Jim to take on the veteran breakfast club and he did. It evolved and developed with Jim doing a marvellous job and he decided to set up his own community interest company. He asked me to be on his board of non-executive directors. However, with my role as the council's Armed Forces Champion, it would be a conflict of interest. I resigned from my role as the champion and it was taken over by Andy Newman, who does a fantastic job. I began supporting Jim with his venture, in the background, there when he needs me. It is an honour, I love what they do at Operation Veteran. They help so many people and I am proud of what Jim has achieved, from nothing.

I feel blessed and have a strong Christian belief, that many people are not aware of and if every day you can be kind and help someone, then job done.

Dedicated to Ian Richardson, a true friend and missed by all who knew him.

In Father's Footsteps
George Edward Woodall (Eddy)

Name: George Edward Woodall (Eddy)
Age: 74 years old
Armed Forces, Regiment / Rank: Territorial Army -
Royal Electrical Mechanical Engineers - Craftsman
Date entered: 1960
Date left: 1970, rejoined 1979 – 1986

My dad was my hero and my inspiration from such a young age. I grew up in the town of Wallsend and attended the local church school, St Peter's. My dad was a server at the church and I joined the church, where I was a choir boy and then a server. My dad eventually became a server in Newcastle Cathedral. Everything he did, I wanted to do. My dad, my best friend, my idol.

I didn't find out more about my dad's time in the army until I was older, but I knew he had served in the Second World War. He was in the Durham Light Infantry and was a sergeant. He served in Egypt and China in the Second World

War then he was captured and taken to a Prisoner of War camp in Germany, in 1943 for one year and seven months. I have a health report from his later life that documents some of these times. It's heartbreaking reading the impact on his well-being from the torture he was subjected to.

SERVICE AFTER 2nd SEPTEMBER, 1939					SERVICE BEFORE 3rd SEPTEMBER, 1939					
Unit	Yrs	Mths	Dates From	To	Unit	Yrs	Mths	Dates From	To
D.L.I.	6	8	3. 9.39	21. 4.46	D.L.I.	1	1	20. 7.38	2. 9.39
Colour Reserve			*BATTALION*		Colour Reserve				
			14th LIGHT INF		Territorial Force	1	4	23. 3.37	19. 7.38

SERVICE ABROAD					CAUSE OF DISCHARGE
Country	Yr.	Mtho	Dates From	To	1938 Having enlisted into Regular Army. 1946 Permanently unfit for any form of Military Service in consequence of 1. Anxiety state (recent, moderate, unspecified). 2. Bilateral otitis externa.
China	-	1	19. 7.39	2. 9.39	
China Egypt Germany (POW)	- 3 1	4 9 7	3. 9.39 7. 1.40 3.10.43	6. 1.40 2.10.43 22. 5.45	

Dad's papers in later life highlight his time as a POW.

My dad was scarred by the Second World War; physically and mentally. He was shot in the head and had his head cut open, carrying the scars all his life. The visible scars that all could see. The pain never left him. In later life, he developed Alzheimer's, which eventually killed him. I asked a few times about what had happened during the War and he told me he couldn't talk about it. He never detailed the horror of what went on for those long days, but we all know. We know of the hate, torture, punishment, execution and barbaric evil that went on in those places and I know my dad wouldn't have been exempt from it. We never knew, my mother never knew.

He complained of headaches all his life. The emotional

scars only he could see, although at times, they crawled out and he would say something or a look in his eyes showed the inner turmoil. Usually, in alcohol, he would get upset and I would know, that the demons that lived in his head, the monsters that ravaged his heart, were never quiet for long. But even with the hate he had witnessed, the hate he had been victim to, my dad was still a kind and loving man. A man I miss each day and my forever hero. It's difficult for me on Remembrance Day and his birthday is also close to that date.

I remember when I was a child, we used to go around the streets selling poppies for the poppy appeal. Door to door salesmen! We would then stand in Wallsend Forum shops on a weekend, selling the poppies there. My dad was so proud and it made me proud to help him. I loved those times, my dad was so passionate about raising money and awareness for our military folk.

I joined the local Royal British Legion group when I was 18 years old, supporting my dad to participate. I used to take my dad to the Armed Forces Association once a month as he got older. It was a pleasure and it made him happy being around his friends, his comrades. Many had served in World War II, some had even served in World War I. Whilst they didn't always talk about the wars, there was an understanding, a blanket of empathy that you could almost feel in the room. The horror stories vaulted away in the minds of all the soldiers as they sat and drank tea and coffee, laughing and joking. My dad needed that, just like the others who attended did. Maybe it helped soothe the trauma so many felt and had carried for so many years.

As with most men from his generation, Dad didn't talk about it. The horror of the War became something that many were silent about as if discussing it would knock down the fragile wall they had built around themselves after the abhorrent destruction of War. A wall to protect themselves mentally, but knowing it was too late in reality. There was no help in those days, not like now. Mental health wasn't discussed and men weren't allowed to cry and ask for help. They didn't talk about what happened and how it impacted them. The ghosts. Instead, men of my dad's generation and my generation just got on with it, the 'stiff upper lip.'

Dad in his Server days, standing, 8ʰ from left.
Me on the front row, 2ⁿᵈ right.

I became an honorary member of the Royal British Legion group and my wife, Irene even got involved when we met, helping with raffles and events. It meant a lot, to my dad and me. The groups gave my dad something to look forward to and it meant we got him out of the house. We would go to Saltwell Park in Gateshead as this is where the monument stands for the Durham Light Infantry, the regiment Dad served in. The War changed my dad, it was irreversible damage, both physically and psychologically. He was never the same, even when my mother was alive. He would forget things and get distressed. But the groups, give him a sense of place, of purpose, of unity with his brothers in arms. My dad passed in 2000, aged 80 years old.

My dad encouraged me to join the forces, telling me it wasn't always about going to war but about learning discipline, transferable skills and being physically and mentally fit. So I joined the Territorial Army when I was 22 years old, completing my training at Borden.

Originally, when I was young, I wanted to go into the RAF but I was married at a young age and life got in the way. I had started working in the Co-op. I enjoyed it and I was going to work my way up to management but then an opportunity came up at the local bus company, where secured a job as a fitter. I served my time and went on to work in different haulage companies. Alongside this, I was working in the TA but it was a lot, working a few jobs and I had a young family. The TA was amazing but I was often away training on weekends, meaning managing family time was challenging. I couldn't attend camp with a young family to look after and ended up leaving the TA after a decade in 1970.

I relished my time in the forces, it wasn't just about the role but also the people you meet. I enjoyed the parades and drills, the routine and self-discipline. We would do target shooting and I achieved the best recruit of the year, my reward being a leather wallet. I gave the wallet to my dad, who was very emotional, crying when I handed it to him. He had told me I was as good as he was and I replied jokingly, "As long as I don't get shot in the head like you, Dad!"

The social side of the TA was also wonderful; dances, dinners and social nights. It was a community within itself and I made so many friends for life. I have many memories of great times. I was there when the Queen opened the Tyne Tunnel in 1967.

I talk to the cadets still and I am part of several associations; I'm president of the local veterans club, involved in the association and vice chair for the British Legion group in the area. These groups at a local level are important. To remember our duty, to support one another locally and to be part of national events such as parades.

Me on parade at Blagdon Hall (2019)

I think National Service should be brought back for young people. Not to send them to war, in another country, but to train them, upskill them and help our young generation to be independent. Some of the life lessons learnt in the forces are principles that stay with you; respect, self-discipline, loyalty, organizational skills, time-keeping. So many essential skills and values for life.

After returning to the TA in 1979 and leaving finally in 1986, I went back to working at the bus company, where I managed the night shift. My driving led me to meet my wife, Irene, 15 years ago. However, it wasn't the first time we had met! When we were both young adults, Irene and I were in the hospital at the same time. Irene was a hairdresser and one day, the nurse asked Irene if she could request her mother brought her hairdressing scissors in when she next visited and if Irene wouldn't mind giving a few of the male patients a haircut. Irene had agreed and she had cut my hair! We both just got on with our lives but our paths were to cross again. When I returned to working on the buses, Irene got a job cleaning the depot. However, we were on separate shifts, so although in the same place, we never saw one another. At this point in our lives, we were both married. Irene worked there for ten years and we never met!

Our paths crossed yet again when Irene was playing darts, as part of a local team. One Sunday, there was a competition and I was the minibus driver, taking them to venues. I was in my late 50s and Irene was 60 years old. I was divorced at the time and Irene's husband had died. There were a few shy smiles and hello's and we were both unsure as to whether the feelings of attraction were mutual or whether it was just friendliness. One time, Irene was going to be the last person getting dropped off after a match. We got a chance and swapped numbers then it all took off from there. I asked Irene where she was next playing darts and I turned up with a bouquet of flowers. We started dating and our relationship hit the bullseye. We got together in the November, I proposed at Christmas and we got married the following August. We were in love, we didn't want to waste time. We are really happy and grateful for another chance of love. It's been a wonderful 15 years together and we hope for many years to come together.

If I were young enough, I would go back into the TA. Irene and I both visit Operation Veteran, so it means Irene has met people and made friends. She is very supportive of me and my groups and commitments with the Legion. It's important to me and for the memory of my dad, as well as all the others that have served.

Me, centre at Queen Elizabeth II memorial service (Sept 2022)

Dedicated to James Edward Jarvis Woodall.

A Girl's Goal
Grace Marie Mcleod

Name: Grace Marie Mcleod
Age: 31 years old
Armed Forces, Regiment / Rank: British Army, Royal Army Medical Core (Corporal)
Conflicts / Tours served: Herrick, Afghanistan. Operation Shader, Iraq and Syria
Date entered: 2007
Date left: 2021 (Still serving in the TA / Reservists)

As a child growing up in Aberdeen, I can't remember wanting to do anything else but join the army. When my friends were having a sleepover and then in later years, having parties and going to raves, I was in the Cadets and I adored it. If I got into trouble and my parents grounded me, the punishment would be that I wasn't allowed to go to Cadets. It was the worst thing that could happen! The Cadets started the military family for me, something I have had throughout my life. A prized possession that I don't think I can ever give up completely.

At school, I got to the age of work experience being

offered. My priority was the military but another love was baking, something I still do today. I was matched a placement in a bakery and I punched the air, excited to be decorating beautiful cakes and baking masterpieces. It was a lot less glamourous, as my placement transpired to be working in a factory making bread rolls. The school I attended then arranged a week-long course, looking at army life. I was first in the queue to sign up and I spent the most brilliant week at Gordon Barracks in Aberdeen. It consolidated that the army was my focus and my destiny.

When I turned 16 years old, I had a few short-term jobs before applying for the army. I remember being at Cadet camp and I received my high school exam grades and my acceptance into the army on the same day. My dream was coming true and my future felt filled with possibility.

Selection commenced; two days of testing in Edinburgh. I passed and was officially part of the army family. My parents were supportive, knowing how much I wanted this. I had been in the Cadets since I was 13 years old and my role in the army would mean learning a trade, getting an education at foundation college and not being in any conflicts or tours posing risk until I was 18 years old. My dad drove me from Aberdeen to the foundation training base, in Harrogate and that was it, I was in the Army.

The first six weeks of training were easy for me as it was similar to my learning with the Cadets. It quickly became more difficult for the remaining ten months. I enjoyed it all, despite the challenges. After phase one training, I progressed to phase two training at Keogh Barracks, for six months of medic training. I passed out in 2009, aged 18 years old, as a class two medic.

My first posting was in Preston and I was fresh into the big army! I was there for four years and it was amazing. We had the normality of young life as the barracks were based in a city. Socialising, nights out and being a young adult. I managed to experience normal young adult life, as well as being a serious medic. There were several times we completed parades half cut, having consumed too much alcohol the night before. I got into trouble with my staff sergeant on more than one occasion with the punishment of work parades such as sweeping leaves from around camp in the rain and being a taxi in the middle of the night. At the time I would swear to never drink again and it would last, for a few days anyway!

During my time in Preston, I was deployed to Afghanistan. The unit I was part of in Preston, Three Med, was to take over Herrick 17, in 2012. We were to spend six months in the desert, in war. I was 21 years old and the army had become very real. There wasn't going to be the comforting blanket of the UK postings, where I could go out partying on the weekend and still do my job, surrounded by safety and my friends. Part of me wanted to go to Afghan, it is what the army was about, defending and protecting. It's why I signed up. But it still felt like the penny of reality had really dropped.

Afghan was indescribably difficult at times. I wondered if life would ever be the same and even if I would survive. Other times I felt such love and camaraderie from my comrade family, that it soothed the most painful of days. I lost one of my closest friends out there, Channing, within a few weeks.

Channing was a 25 year old medic and was killed by the Taliban on her way to teach Afghan soldiers basic medical advice. The person who opened fire on the vehicle she was travelling in was never found. When we were informed of Channing's death, we had little time to grieve. The army is 24/7, there is nowhere to rest, to go, stop and reflect. You work nights, guarding the camp and your comrades. When you sleep, your mind and body is exhausted but still, always on alert, like a gazelle in the wilds of Africa. Alert, always watching for predators and attacks.

Me and Channing, Preston 2012

As medics, we thought that we were protected. We were wrong. We were all vulnerable, like every one of our brave soldiers that worked in Afghanistan. It was the reality of war for me, losing Channing and having to get straight back to work. We were all part of the machine that had to keep going, processing, and ready for action. But we are all human and losing one of our own in a scary place, in horrific, unnecessary circumstances is a kick in the stomach that never goes away.

We did get support from the army and one of our commanding officers brought us all together to talk about Channing's death. He got emotional and it was important to see the humans behind the machine. There was access to support and this made a difference, as I know historically there hasn't always been mental health support in the forces.

We may have been soldiers first, but we were people, with feelings and fears. Comrades were supportive but due to our position, we had to bottle our grief in some ways. It never went away. It remained, fizzing and bubbling under the surface as we continued to be part of the machine. Myself and seven other comrades got to carry her coffin onto the plane, a final goodbye, sending her back to her family. After Channing died, I double-checked everything and became super vigilant. The reality was that none of us were immune. It has ten years this year since Channing was killed, but it feels like yesterday. The loss of a fellow soldier but also a treasured friend. I think of her every day. What she would be doing now, the future she never got. Our memories together, her bravery, our laughs. Never forgotten.

We spent Christmas 2012 in Afghanistan. It was the hardest time of year for many of us, but the army made a great effort. There was a carol service on Christmas Eve and nice food, parcels from home and parcels from a company filled with treats. The army gave us a lie-in on Christmas Day and we were allowed to wear Santa hats instead of berets for the day. It was lovely then we had a fun run, some games and a meal together. We missed our families, but we had our forces family and made it a wonderful day.

Me at Christmas, in Afghanistan (2012)

During our time in Afghanistan, shows and entertainment were also on offer. Bands and celebrities would come out and visit. It felt really special and even more so that they were travelling out for us, to show gratitude, lift our morale and entertain us. One time Daniel Craig came out and we got a free screening of his latest Bond film, Skyfall. It was an amazing night. We had visits from the Prime Minister at the time, David Cameron and Cheryl Cole also visited us. I remember fondly one night, the entertainers had us all on our feet dancing to The Harlem Shake. It was brilliant fun and is on YouTube still! It was times like that where we felt normal and hopeful. For a few hours got a chance to try and forget the horror that was going on around us. Some respite from reality.

Prince Harry or as he was known, Captain Wales, was in Afghanistan when I was on tour. I didn't work with him personally, but one day myself and friends went to the canteen and there were no seats. Captain Wales and his crew saw us looking for seats and they all got up, offering us their places. I sat in his chair and had a happy, child-like grin on my face all night! It was surreal and I was a little starstruck, but

Captain Wales was one of us in Afghan, doing his part to protect and defend.

During my time in camp, we would go out with the vehicle patrols, delivering supplies to checkpoints, as backup in case of an incident requiring medical assistance. I also completed a stint with the ambulance crew for Camp Bastion. We would drive to the helicopter landing area called Nightingale and transport casualties. This was a daily occurrence and the casualties weren't just British soldiers, they were from everywhere, and included people who had been injured as a result of us. For example, if a civilian got caught up in an attack and it wasn't their fault. I experienced my first fatality as a medic in this role. I remember it was an American contractor, a close protection officer who had been shot dead. We took his body off the helicopter and he lay on the stretcher, his body was covered. However, the rotors of the helicopter were still spinning around and the wind from this movement rippled through the cover over the man, making it flap, leading to his face being exposed. As we transported him to the morgue, I just couldn't stop thinking about the material that was meant to be covering him, but instead was exposing him. That he was someone's son, perhaps partner, brother and father. It still stays with me now and I can still hear the sound of the material.

Another time I was working to support healthcare in the prisons. There were prisons on site that housed prisoners of war, and terrorist detainees. Under the Geneva Convention, the prisoners were entitled to medical assistance. Myself and a doctor would go out every morning, checking in with the prisoners and asking if they had any health concerns. One day the ambulance service received an emergency call. Some detainees had broken out of the prison whilst a team of engineers had been working on site, installing a mesh cover over the prison. Prisoners had managed to grab the engineer's tools; spanners, hammers, metal tools and had assaulted the soldiers. One engineer had been assaulted so badly, he was in a coma and returned home to England. I'm not sure if he even survived. It was an extremely difficult day and on days like that, it was hard to keep your ethics, values and emotions in check. But that's what the British Army does. We stick to the rules, the Geneva Convention and that's why we are one of the best in the world. We had to do our job, treat the prisoners as humans; treat them medically, feed them and allow them to pray. It was our job, it's what we did.

On my return from Afghan, I was posted to Abingdon, Oxford-shire, attached to the Royal Logistics. I remained here for 2-3 years, had my own little room and en-suite and during this time, I was promoted to corporal before being posted to Catterick with 5 Med, in 2015. When I got back from Afghanistan, we had a medals parade. My family were there and my heart felt full. It

3 medical regiment medals parade for Herrick 17, Catterick Garrison (2013)

was my first medal and receiving it made me feel all the bad times were almost worthwhile. I am proud of my Afghan medal – anyone who has been to Afghan knows you earn that medal!

In 2015, I began a posting at Catterick. I was less keen on this posting, it was a mainstream unit and felt stricter. I did however, buy my first house in Catterick, through army and government help. This was wonderful for me and meant I could commute to work and have a much better work-life balance. I got a dog, Pippa, who I still have now.

Iraq 2016-2017

I went on tour in 2016 to Iraq and Syria, when ISIS was at large. We were asked by the Iraqi government to teach the soldiers how to go to war. They had an established military but needed some assistance. This was strange as during the first Iraq war, we were fighting them. I was there for six months and there were no problems. My role was to teach medical awareness and safety. Culturally, it was difficult. The soldiers were all male and had to learn from me as a female. However, they were respectful and understood that our culture was not theirs and that I was teaching them as a qualified, professional medic. I helped teach them the skills needed to save each other's lives. ISIS was taking over parts of their country and the overall training we offered, including weapons training, engineering and from our team, the skills were to reduce mortality in battle. Our team's training supported the soldier's practice and reduced the mortality rate by approximately 20%. I enjoyed the tour and we also worked with the Australian and New Zealand Army. When we left, the New Zealand Army performed a Haka to their handover unit and it was magnificent to watch.

Me, Iraq, 2016-2017

I remained at Catterick on my return from Iraq, but became attached to another unit, Two Yorks, based in the medical centre. This was my unit until I left the army in 2021. Not long after being posted with Two Yorks, we went on exercise for a month where we slept out for two weeks in our ambulance, with rations. I think this was the start of the end for me.

When I signed off from the army, I wasn't in a great place. I felt unsettled and a relationship I was in had just broken down. I felt fed up and I impulsively signed off with the hope of going into the property sector. I had a year of resettlement and achieved my project management qualification and then

Covid hit. I was due to join a firm in Glasgow, which ran an ex-forces programme of training with the end result being a job in project management. However, it didn't materialise due to Covid. I was worried about security and income, so I accepted a job in Newcastle with a private ambulance service. I had friends in Newcastle so that was a pull for me. I immediately disliked the job. Then I caught Covid on my first week in the role and suffered badly. I never returned to the job, feeling it wasn't right for me.

Me, with my Iraq medal, 2019

Not long after, I met my partner Mel and moved in with her a few months later. I had joined the Reservists and secured an administration job. The Reservists is perfect for me; I still have the camaraderie and forces family, but I can pick and choose what I do with the Reservists, to a degree. It also means I have a life that is manageable in civvy street. I have a wonderful partner, a lovely home and great friends. I am at a crossroads in my career, but I know it will all fall into place and I am grateful for everything the army taught me and for helping to shape the person I am today. I made friends that I still keep in touch with now, friends that are more than friends, they are family and will always be with me, even those in spirit.

Dedicated to Channing Day.

'Man Up!'
Heather Margaret Perkins

Name: Heather Margaret Perkins
Age: 33 years old
Armed Forces, Regiment / Rank: RAF, 7 Squadron, Chinooks, Mechanical Engineer
Conflicts / Tours served: Afghanistan (2011-2012)
Date entered: 2009
Date left: 2013

I wanted to be in the RAF from a young age. It felt like a calling and my grandfather had served in the RAF, as an engineer. My grandad was an inspiration to me and our bond was more like a father and daughter, as I didn't have that relationship with my dad. My brother is also part of the armed forces, a para-trooper. He used to say to me that I wasn't joining the army because I was a girl, so the RAF felt like a natural pull.

It was really daunting going into my local RAF careers office at 19 years old, but I went along, in the hope to be a photographer. They told me they did not require photographers but were in need of engineers. There was a stark difference between what I wanted to do and the offer there and then of engineering. The armed forces is a male-dominated world. Not many women want to go into engineering and even less in the military. I didn't have GCSEs and told them I hadn't even touched a spanner before, but they advised me I would receive training and support. Grandad was my world, my hero and perhaps the offer of being an engineer in the RAF was my destiny. My nan was also in the air force and from their stories over the years, I knew they were better than superheroes. I wanted to make them proud of me, like the pride and admiration I held for them both from such a young age.

Me, with my grandparents, the night I returned from Afghanistan

The decision was made. I was joining the RAF as an engineer. After phase one basic training, I went on to phase two, more specialised training. This taught me a range of engineering skills and alongside this, we continued learning skills to defend and attack. I remember vividly one training exercise where we were trained to manage a gas attack. We basically had to go into a gas chamber, where CS tablets were distributed and we had to take off our gas masks. I remember my eyes and nose streaming, like the life inside of me was melting and pouring out all of my orifices. It was hideous and when I got out, I felt so desperate for a cuddle and some comfort from a loved one. I just wanted my mum. I was soon back into reality, screamed at by my sergeant for touching my face and ordered to run around the trees outside.

I was so young and even when I was learning such detailed precision, massive risk management and life-saving techniques, emotionally, I felt like a child at times. It was hard, to stay strong when you feel vulnerable. To not have home comforts, routines and familiarity. To not have friends or family and that closeness of a hug or a tender arm touch when you need soothing human contact.

There was always something scary to try and overcome. The creeping feeling of dread and fear that I constantly had to smoother. Through achieving the challenges, conquering physically and emotionally excruciating times, it has made me the person I am. But it was so hard and I found it harder as a female. Not just physically and emotionally, but culturally.

After passing out and completing my year of training in phase two, I was posted straight to Seven Squadron, Chinooks. Within a month of being at Chinooks, I was told I was going to be posted to Oman. I felt thrown in at the deep end but this was what I had joined for and the excitement in me soon became empowering. This was my first ever detachment from home.

I was chosen to work on helicopters and for a long while, I

was the only female there, which felt strange in many ways. The men tried to include me and I had a good sense of humour and an adaptable personality. But there were still significant differences and as much I tried to be 'one of the lads,' there was always that evident divide in many ways. I felt that some of the engineers thought women shouldn't be engineers and the other females on camp, who were in more office roles, saw me as 'manly.' I never felt like I fitted in anywhere.

Despite that, I did make friends and the family side of the air force was amazing, as many other people in the military would say. I still miss them to this day. Our family got through Afghan, Oman and America together. During heartbreaking times, that still upset me now, my RAF family was there. When it really mattered, when things felt like we would never survive, never get home, never smile again – they were there and I will be grateful for eternity for that.

I completed my tour in Afghan, a winter tour 2011-2012. I was there for Christmas 2011, new year and my birthday. I turned 22 years old in Afghanistan and although it is still very young, I didn't feel young by this point in my career. Some of the nicest times we had in the RAF were in the worst places. In the middle of the desert, hot and irritated, with no home comforts. It didn't matter where we were, the military family made it for you, usually with humour! One time in Afghan, something happened to my face. It began drooping and I couldn't speak, drool slithering from the corner of my mouth. For the first five minutes, the lads were making fun of me, laughing and pointing. Then one of the sergeants said he thought I needed to go to the hospital. Everything was ok at the hospital but this summed up the forces, that humour and laughing at one another, even sometimes in serious conditions. The mocking and playful joking made you a family. You could never get away with it in civvy street, but it was affection in the forces. I've never found that anywhere else.

Another time still haunts me in my sleep. I remember on new year's eve in Afghan at 4 am. Our squadron were told we were conduction a re-patriation. A marine captain had been killed after driving over an IED. The Herc plane was coming in and we were to be on parade. The silence was deafening. Normally there would be noise, something; an explosion, rockets going off, vehicles and aircrafts landing. But it was silent, our breathing the only sound. I remember standing there at 4 am thinking the captain was returning to the UK, to his family, in a coffin. I recall praying in my head that no rockets would go off, no attack and for the time to remain silent. Silence to give our fallen comrade his time, his moment and our respect. The Herc landed and we placed our comrade's coffin on the plane before it quickly took off again. Literally, within the space of a few seconds, the roar of the helicopter broke that silence and then it was straight back to work. We never talked about it, we never got a chance. We just went back to work, like the machines we had become.

It comes back to me sometimes, in the quiet of the night, haunting me. I often think of his family and the lives that were taken, his and my other fallen comrades. I never met that captain in person, but I carry a marine cap badge on me and I've been to the memorial wall where his name is. Whenever I have a drink, I raise a toast to him and our other soldiers lost in battle.

I began having nightmares and struggling in the RAF. I was given anti-psychotic medication and then told I wasn't fit for service. I was discharged and out of the air force within a month. There were no offers of support given, no checking whether I had somewhere to live, a job or monitoring of my wellbeing. Luckily, I had my mum for support and to offer a roof over my

head. Some people don't have that and we have so many veterans on the streets or in prison with mental ill health and addiction issues.

Me, planting poppy crosses for Remembrance Sunday

In the forces, as soon as you enter and take off the comfortable slippers of civvy street, you are told to 'man up!' Alongside this, you are told to laugh about things. It is a coping mechanism. The military is so good at teaching you how to be a soldier and how to 'man up,' but when you leave the forces, you aren't taught how to be a civilian again. Your whole personality has altered. Everything you do and the reasons are different within the forces compared to life outside. Civvy street is like stepping into another world, a world you've been in before but a world that now feels alien.

When I got back home, I looked at my friends who were civilians and felt so much older than them. My experiences, training, and the military family, had all made me grow up. It highlighted the disparity between us. Almost strangers and it was sad. History became all I had in common with lots of friends. I tried to talk about parts of my military life, the parts I felt I could, but my friends just didn't understand and would look at me as if I were speaking another language. In a way, I guess I was. Other parts I couldn't talk about. What I had seen, parts that haunted me, like a soul sickness. It had changed me forever and I felt so isolated.

With nothing in common in the here and now with my old friends, it was hard to keep the connection. Alongside their understandable lack of appreciation of the emotional impact of war. They tried to empathise, but with anything, you can only imagine to a degree and the reality of war is something only understood by those trapped or fighting it.

That first year back in civvy street was so hard for me. At times I felt like I was drowning. My head would bob above the tide when something good happened, a simple thing like a nice afternoon without feeling emotionally fraught, or a good night's sleep. Then the waves of anxiety, fear, uncertainty, worthlessness and feeling lonely in a room full of people would pull me back down, under the water, squeezing the breath out of me. It felt like I would never be okay again and I missed my military family, the only people I felt understood me. I'd lost my family. I'd lost my friends. I felt invisible and alone.

I was diagnosed with manic depression, PTSD and traumatic amnesia. I struggled to get out of bed, I couldn't work, didn't want to see anyone and felt I would never feel 'normal,' again. But slowly I started to heal and I began to realise I never wanted anyone to feel how I felt at my lowest.

There isn't enough money and resources for supporting veterans. When I left, I was offered nothing. No support, no signposting and that was less than a decade ago. For years and years people have left the military damaged, with no way of healing, no tools and support to get better and live a healthy and happy life. I also had the feeling that "I was only an engineer" and felt I didn't deserve help as I wasn't a soldier. When I went to regular services for support, doors were closed on me with the excuse of services not specializing in veteran support. I had to do it myself. I remember one day, staring at my reflection in the mirror after a morning of struggling to get out of bed and it clicked, I had to do it. The only person that could help me, was me. So I did. It wasn't easy, I had setbacks but I found that determined woman who was a determined young girl, wanting to join the RAF and not giving up. I found her and she found me again.

I began taking small steps in the right direction to have a future, a fulfilling future. I secured a job at Marks and Spencer as an engineer. I realised they employed a lot of veterans and reservists, although we didn't have a veterans network. I spoke with the CEO about setting up a social network and he agreed, supporting me with the idea. I created a logo and set up the support group virtually, super excited to be doing something that could benefit colleagues but also help me. At the first meeting, it was just me, talking to no one! But I refused to give up. I kept it going and within a few months, almost all of the veterans had joined. I became chair and we were able to achieve so much. The most important thing was that people had someone to talk to, to understand. They would ring me themselves when they were struggling or a colleague would ring me to say someone was having a panic attack. We would talk through things and help people understand.

A few months ago I left Marks and Spencer to move to the North East. It felt like I was leaving my military family again, with a heavy heart. The key reason I wanted to establish veterans support at Marks and Spencer was that all veterans will struggle at some point. They may

Me, whilst working at Marks & Spencer

transition back to civvy street relatively easily and re-immerse themselves into society; working and managing family life.

But then something can happen, the smallest of things that can be the catalyst of destruction. To suddenly realise you are alone and surrounded by people who do not understand is gut-wrenching. Networks that connect veterans can make such a huge difference. I didn't have one when I left the RAF, but the one I created at Marks and Spencer helped me so much and led to me starting a career working with veterans. I think part of me will always feel alone, but I am trying to make it as small a part as I can.

I moved to Newcastle, securing a job with Walking with the Wounded, after connecting with them through Marks and Spencer. I travelled from my hometown in the south of the country a few months ago. The people in Newcastle are lovely, it feels like home already. I manage my wellbeing now and know how to keep myself healthy. I love my job and I visit Operation Veteran when I can. The beach walks are wonderful and even though many of us have served at very different times, the connection is there. They have become my friends and part of my life.

Working at Walking with the Wounded means I am attached to the forces community again and helps me to keep as well as I can. It doesn't matter which armed forces you served in, what your rank was, how old you are, or how you identify, there is a common bond, an unbreakable bond. I want to encourage more organisations to become forces friendly and to understand the younger veteran. Many people would describe a veteran as an elderly man or a Chelsea Pensioner, which of course is true, but there are many younger veterans and female veterans. Alongside younger veterans, we have modern issues. It isn't about 'manning up,' we need to understand veterans, our diversity and our needs. The military is really good at offering support to people with physical injuries, perhaps because you can see a broken back or lost limb. But mental health support has a long way to go and I hope in my role at Walking with the Wounded, I can help change this, even in the smallest of ways.

Me, at Operation Veteran's Queen Elizabeth II memorial (Sept 2022)

Dedicated to Marine Captain Tom Jennings and to all the 457 heroes we lost in Afghanistan. Stand easy, your time in hell is done.

Born to Do This
James (Jim) Owens

Name: James (Jim) Owens
Age: 60 years old
Armed Forces, Regiment / Rank: RAF, Aircrafts
Weapons Technician / Armourer
Conflicts / Tours served: The Falklands
Date entered: 1980
Date left: 1990

I was the oldest of six kids, growing up in the tenements of
Glasgow. We struggled with poverty, like many households
around us. My family lived in a two roomed tenement, with
no central heating and a shared outside toilet, used by three
other families. It was hard growing up and my parents did the
absolute best they could. We didn't have much, but we always
had each other and books. We were all avid readers and I have
some lovely memories of reading times in our family. My role
in the household, as the oldest child, was to help with the
young children. Alongside this, I would babysit other families'

children, throughout my young adulthood. I became mature, independent and determined at an early age.

When I was 12 years old, we moved to Nottingham, with my dad securing work at Raleigh Bikes. I attended a grammar school, managing to stay in the top sets. Despite this, I left school with no qualifications. I applied to join the RAF but was advised I had nothing to offer skill wise. I was told to go away and learn a skill that could be utilized or developed in the RAF at a later date.

Mum, me and some of my siblings, Glasgow.

I obtained a job at a tailoring factory for three months, followed by a role as a driver's mate. Then, I worked for 18 months in a tannery, as my dad worked in the leather industry at the time. One day, I was standing at my machine, chilled to the bone as I looked. The factory was filled with men who had worked there for decades, knowing little else, who had no further dreams and would stay in the tannery forever. Their bones were tired and contorted from the strenuous work in a cold environment, with inadequate breaks and no care for wellbeing from the superiors.

I wanted to scream inside, I could almost see myself watching my life trickle down the plughole. I needed to do something about it, life had to be more than this. I had been reading Wilbur Smith and other authors who talked about adventure and travelling the world. In the January of 1980, I went back to the RAF, at 18 years old and completed all the tests. I was offered to enter as a mechanic and was told by a sergeant armourer that armourers were 'God's chosen few.' A big, appealing picture was painted and I felt like a child on their birthday. I had signed up before the sergeant had finished speaking.

By March 1980, my call came to say I was in. I handed in my notice that week at work, asking my supervisor not to tell my dad. I returned home and my mum queried why I wasn't at work. I informed her I was joining the RAF and she asked "When?"

I replied, "Tomorrow."

Without blinking, she told me I wasn't going. I was 18 years old, it was up to me and I said that to her. I was her oldest child, but I was also a massive help in the house. My mum worked nights, 12 hour shifts five nights a week as a night nurse. I took my siblings to school, played sports with them after school and helped cook and clean. I was a major part of the running of the house.

My dad was more encouraging as he had been in the RAF for three years, two of which were National Service. He talked about the RAF all my life. When my dad got home that evening, my mum told him what I wanted to do. He shook my hand and gave his blessing telling my mum it was the RAF or a life on the factory floor. Ironically, the morning I was due to leave for the RAF, someone knocked on the door to offer me an apprenticeship mechanic role – a job I had gone for three months earlier. At that moment, I had to make a life changing decision, in a split second, as an 18 year old. I went with my heart, the RAF.

So off I went, doing my six weeks of training at RAF Swinderby, Lincolnshire. I was already physically fit and had been practicing martial arts for several years as well as playing football. This helped me adjust quickly to the intense physical workouts in my training. I was also used to a room full of people, coming from a big family. However, what I wasn't used to was being shouted at and beds being tipped over in a heartbeat. My dad had given me advice to not take things personally in the forces. That the forces purpose is to transform us from civilians to military and that in years to come, I would look back and realise that, despite the anger I may feel at the time.

We began wearing our uniform, part of the transforming process. On the first night, we were allowed to go for a few alcoholic drinks. On our return, we were advised there would be a 'mineval' a minimum evaluation of how we respond in a wartime situation. It was 2 am and we were all in bed, worse for wear when sirens began going off. We all jumped out of bed and a corporal came in screaming for us to get dressed and stand at the end of our bed. It was a poor performance, given the number of beers we had consumed. After about an hour, we were still there, more swaying than standing, wondering if it was a bad nightmare. We were then told by another corporal, given we had just arrived, there was little we could do and we could lie on top of our beds. Relieved, we all fell onto our beds, embracing the scratchy blankets and went to sleep. Rest wasn't to be and 15 minutes later, the first corporal came back in, blaring like a fog horn, screaming abuse at us to get back up. Eventually, the exercise ended at around 5 am. Thirty minutes later it was morning call and we were up again, what a welcome to the RAF!

Basic training was six weeks then we passed out. My parents and brother came on the day. This was our first major achievement and we all felt so proud, well those who made it through the training. I felt ten feet tall as I began to march. This was my dream, my future.

Basic training (1980), me, front row, second from left

My next posting was RAF Cosford, Wolverhampton, for my aircraft weapons mechanics training. All the indoor sporting and athletics were at Cosford. Any sport you wanted to participate in, you could there. Comms training and PTI training were also based here, so it was a massive base with lots of military folk from across the world completing their training. I spent four and a half months here and the exams had an 80% pass mark to progress. It was intense but necessary for the level of detail, knowledge and skills needed. We would strip down aircraft cannons into 140-150 parts and rebuild them. They needed to be exact. If we dropped a part or tool, we were discovered and punishment was to carry a 40lb barrel around the room, with everyone laughing and pointing. We were all human; error happens but the training was to minimise this. Mistakes meant life or death in the forces and especially when dealing with explosives. If you were working in a cockpit and dropped a part, it could be the tiniest of parts but the plane would be grounded. Or if in the air and something happens, it could result in a fatality.

After passing my training, I was posted to RAF Wittering Cambridge, in the bomb dump. It was the biggest bomb dump site in Europe and my site mainly had cluster bombs and thousand-pound bombs. On arrival, I was handed a paintbrush. The bombs had to be painted as they were cast iron. They were in their thousands and I spent the first six months painting 4-foot-long bombs. My eager enthusiasm like a child going to a funfair, quickly evaporated when the paintbrush became the weapon I didn't want! In the end, I went to my chief and said I could have stayed in civvy street painting. I was put in another bomb dump for a short while, filled with boxes that needed to be checked and stamped as free from explosives, then sealed. This became my next monotonous groundhog day. There was another job in this bomb dump, driving the rough terrain forklifts. I managed to get one of the corporals to teach me how to drive them and got signed up as a forklift driver. My day became more enjoyable as I would rush in and get on a forklift and spend the day driving them.

After 18 months of this however, I was losing my patience. I went to see the warrant officer in charge of all the Armourers. He told me I would be on the OCU (Operational Conversion Unit) at 6 am the next morning. My role would be working on Harrier Jump jets, where the new pilots would be training to fly the plane as a weapon loaded with ammunition. I was fully trained and had to hit the ground running. I had to inspect the aircraft, the ejection seats and the pins, to ensure safety for parking and take off, remove and replace weapons, and marshal the aircraft out and back in. I was in my element.

One morning, I was lying under a harrier at 6 am, fitting 4-lb bombs. It smelt of fuel and was pitch black, cold and raining, but at that moment, I felt like king of the world. It was what I had wanted for so long. As my colleague moaned next to me, his voice disappeared into the cold air as I smiled to myself and knew I was born to do this.

I was on the OCU for six months then we received notification that the Argentinians had invaded the Falklands. We didn't even know where the Falklands were, thinking it was off the coast of Scotland and wondering why the Argentinians were there. We were informed we would be going to the Falklands but were not allowed to tell anyone, including our comrades. We were issued WWII leftover equipment, such as webbing and kit we could use.

My only previous detachment was in Denmark for a month, where early on I met a local woman and went to her house. I woke up the next day in a strange house wondering how a young girl could afford such a lovely home and in awe of the Danish lifestyle. Then there was a clattering about and as her bedroom door opened. It transpired it was her father and as my heart began racing and I wondered how I could grab my belongings and run, he smiled and offered me breakfast. I was welcomed as part of their family, temporarily. So whilst I would be on-site, at the base camp through the day, on an evening I would spend time with my new girlfriend and her father. I would enjoy nice meals, a warm bed and getting my clothes laundered. Quite the opposite of rolling around in the mud at the campsite and sleeping in cold, stinking tents with sodden clothes. One day the sergeant pulled me to one side and enquired as to whether I thought it was acceptable swanning off with my new girlfriend and her father, whilst my comrades were slumming it, doing what we were all here to do; learn how to live in a field. I politely pointed out that I was coming to work on time and doing my duties and with that, the conversation ended.

It was unclear how long we would be out in the Falklands but a date had been decided. By this time, my family was living in Nottingham and I used to travel home every weekend. I went with some of the lads into Nottingham one day as we were off. We decided to buy some equipment to take with us, such as knives, not knowing what to expect at the Falklands. I popped in to see my mum and she asked where I was going. I told her I couldn't say, but she knew. She hugged me, something my mum didn't do and as we left, I saw her sobbing. Her oldest son, going off to war.

After some toing and froing, we eventually got on our way to the Falklands. Many of the lads were seasick, having never been on boats. It didn't help that our vessel to go to war was a car ferry! We travelled through the tropics, which were wonderful but the days were long. We were only allowed two cans of beer a day, whereas higher ranks were allowed four cans and wines and spirits. We soon learnt to request the non-drinkers to get their beers and share them, giving us an increase in stock and a better night all around!

*On our car ferry (The St.
Edmund's), travelling to war
(1982). Me, front, centre.*

We soon arrived at Ascension Island, the sun was rising and I remember seeing it creep up behind a volcano. It was stunning. We restocked and refuelled at Ascension, ready to get on our way. A few days later, the weather turned treacherous. We would sit at food times, hugging our trays and cups to stop them from sliding off the table as the boat rocked over the vicious waves. Food began running out, but we had a massive amount of gammon steak, which became all we ate. We began giving the Gurkhas beer in exchange for curry, to escape the morning, lunch and dinner menu of gammon steak.

Conditions began to worsen and we weren't allowed out on deck due to the weather. The reality of our position became real. We had no anti-aircraft protection and The Atlantic Conveyor, our sister ship a few miles away was hit. Some lives were lost and this ship had our ammunition on board. In that period we had sunk the Argentinian Belgrano, the enemies ship. A 200 mile exclusion was declared around The Falklands. Other boats had been struck and it all felt too close for comfort. Eventually, we came into Port Stanley Sound, just as the Argentines surrendered. Our role was to bring our soldiers back, the Scots Guards, who had trench foot and frostbite. They had been sleeping in holes in the ground; peat ground, filled with icy water and in freezing conditions. Port Stanley was covered in weapons that had been dumped when the Argentines surrendered. We set up our camp, simple tents in horrendous conditions. The Royal Marines helped us as we didn't have the experience. On the first night,

I was on guard duty. Even in my sleeping bag, it felt like going outside with no clothes on. There was a blizzard, it was pitch black and there was gunfire and explosions in the background. We weren't sure if it was still the Argentines, not knowing they had surrendered.

It felt like I imagined hell to be, only on the opposite end of the temperature scale! At that moment I remember thinking I didn't want to die 8,000 miles from home and get buried here. An icy slap of reality in my face and I was frightened. Over the next few days, we set up the

Our tented accommodation, Port Stanley, The Falklands (1982)

bomb dump. Alongside the hard work in freezing cold, winds with peat earth beneath your feet, there were some highs. We were supplied our food and alcohol and bent the truth at issuing, receiving more supplies than our allocated numbers. We would use this as leverage for swaps, mainly to get more alcohol. The simple things made a massive difference in difficult circumstances.

The Hercules planes arrived each day, delivering mail from home. It was our highlight and we all waited like a dog for its favourite treat, daily for our letters from home. Sometimes, comrades didn't get a letter, so we would pass ours round to give them something to read and smile about. Those letters meant the world and sharing the joy was a lovely experience. It brought us closer, our military family. I still have some that my mum wrote to me and my brother has the ones I sent to my mum, as she has sadly passed away.

I remember a very traumatic day, a disaster that occurred when two harrier planes were getting ready for flight. There must have been a fault, as the Sidewinder missiles from one of the aircraft jettisoned immediately after its wheels left the ground. One of the Sidewinder's guidance control systems went haywire and I watched it, in what felt almost slow motion, going out of control and heading towards the runway crossing point where soldiers were standing. They dispersed, and the missile carried on towards them, breaking up and passing through where the troops were. Screaming became the horrifying music in the air as bodies lay on the ground and the smell of fuel and burning skin hit us with pungent nausea. Smoke covered the area.

We rushed down to administer first aid. We were always told to go to the quiet ones as the screaming ones were still alive. Someone took control and quickly helicopters arrived and injured comrades were taken to hospital. Quickly, there was silence, just remains of blood in the snow and smoke in the air. Screams still rang in my ears for some time afterwards. Incidents were never discussed, we had to just carry on with our roles, business as usual. For a long time after this accident, I felt like my mind had played tricks on me as if I was watching a film and not a real-life incident. Luckily, no one died but there were many life-changing injuries; lost limbs, disability and mental scarring. I don't think I ever had PTSD from my time in the RAF but there were definitely disturbing times that I thought about for a long time after and still do on occasion.

There were great times also. On one of our R&R week-ends, we had a break on the SS Rangetera. This meant we could have a good wash, launder our clothes and sleep in a warm, dry, comfortable bed for a few nights. It was bliss and a much-needed break from the damp coldness of the peat. There were four of us in a cabin and I remember one of the lads had a cassette player and headphones. I asked what he was listening to, it was Judie Tzuke, "Stay With me Til Dawn." I said I liked that song and the lad handed me his cassette player, telling me he was going to sleep. I remember listening to the song over and over all night. Each time I hear it now, it reminds me of that night in the RAF, where all the hardship and fear that I had felt for months melted into a memorable moment of gratitude, pride and happiness.

We were in the Falklands for four and a half months in total. Luckily, we travelled home by plane, rather than a boat. I arrived home and my family wanted to make a big deal of my return to Nottingham. We went to the bars in town and all my friends and family joined in the celebrations. After a few days, I was overwhelmed with the constant, "What was it like?" I didn't want to answer and I felt trapped. After less than three weeks, I couldn't take anymore and went back to camp early. When I returned to camp, so many comrades were there, all returning early. Home now felt like the RAF for everyone. It was the place we didn't have to explain or answer the "What was it like?" It felt safe, even when our lives had been at risk so many times.

After The Falklands, I was selected for technician training, before being posted to RAF Wyton, Cambridgeshire. I also had detachments in Germany, Scotland, Cyprus and Norway, which were wonderful and I am grateful for my experiences travelling the world with the RAF.

I eventually left the RAF in 1990, in my late 20s. I remember walking out of the base and thinking I was free, only for the coin to be flipped almost immediately as I realised I no longer had an ID pass and wouldn't be allowed back in. 10 years of my life and now the gate was shut. I had no job, no home and no idea what I could do. I stayed with my mum for a while, who was living in the countryside at the time. I started working at a local steelworks, then a dairy. They didn't work out, my heart wasn't in it and it was never enough for me. I got on a bus to Nottingham centre one day and didn't go back to my mum's. I had no job, no accommodation, and no direction but I knew I needed more than a mundane job that crushed my soul. I began sofa surfing at friends and was drinking an unhealthy amount of alcohol. I slowly started mixing with alcoholics and drug users, petty criminals and then gangsters.

I spent some time staying with a woman I met, as friends. We didn't see much of each other in the first few weeks and she spent a lot of time out of the house. I soon found out she was a drug addict and a sex worker, staying there became too much of a risk so I ended up in a hostel in Nottingham, where I lived for over a year. At the time, I began door-to-door sales. I would go and buy a load of cleaning materials and household items, put my smart clothes on, not have a drink that morning and go around the streets, knocking on doors. I had my sales patter to a tee and even had a photo from a mate of mine, who had four kids in their school uniform. I asked for it and would knock on people's doors telling them I had just left the RAF and was trying to feed my kids, showing them the heart-melting photo. It worked and my sales were soaring and at least half of my act was true!

However, I still returned each night to a dump of a bedroom, in a hostel full of people who had unmet needs, vulnerabilities or who would attack you in the blink of an eye. I wanted out and at this time I was doing well, eating well, working and not drinking alcohol. Then I met a girl and she was an alcoholic with a traumatic backstory. She was also in the hostel and things got out of control, leading to us being asked to leave the accommodation. I was homeless again. Another friend was on 'the run,' in Nottingham. He offered for us to go to the North East with him, to stay at his girlfriend's in Sunderland. We all travelled up but soon my girlfriend couldn't cope and wanted her old environment and drinking associates from Nottingham. Alcohol was her priority, so she returned and sadly later died from her addiction. I remained in Sunderland and there was an incident where my friend on 'the run,' was involved in an undercover drugs investigation. He was lured to Liverpool for a big drug deal and police arrested him and others, resulting in a seven-year prison sentence for possession with intent to supply and possession of a firearm. He had wanted me to go with him to Liverpool, saying it was a trip away and avoiding the real purpose. I had a pool match that night, so I declined, otherwise I would have gone for a lad's day away. I could have been facing that time in prison, had I agreed and gone along.

I was homeless again and met a local girl in Sunderland who was a recovering addict. She had been on heroin since the age of 14 years old and was on a methadone recovery programme when I met her. At first, I thought all would be ok with her, she was engaging with support services and seemed focused. However, as with the dark side of addiction, the demons resurfaced and she began using, lying and getting involved with undesirable people. She was unpredictable when on drugs and would often be aggressive and violent. I had another friend in the area who was a solvent abuser and would sniff lighter fuel. I didn't even know it was a thing but it was his 'high' of choice. One day he came round and told us he had been in the police station all night. His 15-year-old nephew had come to his house, found the gas, inhaled and died instantly from a heart attack. A tragedy and a massive alarm bell that I needed to get out, away from this scene. But alcohol and the knowledge I had nowhere to go, kept me there.

Things got worse and soon myself and my girlfriend split up. I remained in the house, waiting to find somewhere else to go and looking after her dog. I think part of me wanted to try and help her. One night she stayed out all night and came back the next morning. In a confrontational manner, she started asking me questions. I could tell she was intoxicated and she seemed full of fury, a fire of rage around her getting stronger as she spoke. I calmly tried to leave the room we were in, to get away from the friction and she inflicted a frenzied assault on me with a belt and dog chain. I managed to leave the property, my face cut and bleeding and vowed to never return. Sadly, she later died from an overdose, another fatality to substance misuse.

I was homeless. I had nothing and no one. I was in my early 30s and felt worthless. I walked into Sunderland centre the following day, not sure where I was going or what I would do on my arrival. It was a cold, rainy day and as it got dark, I didn't know where to turn. I spent the night sleeping in a doorway, knowing I had reached rock bottom. Life didn't even feel worth living. I wasn't living, I was existing and it was a painful, lonely existence. I ended up going to the local police station to ask for help. They directed me to an accommodation service, who turned me away at the door. They pointed me in the direction of a hostel, which was notorious for accommodating homeless people, many problematic. The caretaker said I would have to come back in the morning, so I returned to the police station. By this time it was about 4 am, I was exhausted, hungry, cold and soaking wet. I was allowed to sit down, then five minutes later a sergeant on duty came by and told me to get out. I mentioned I was ex-forces but it made no difference and I left. I wasn't causing any problems, just trying to get warm and rest. Maybe I should have just put a brick through a window and got arrested for the night. At least then I would have had somewhere to sleep and some food.

I was in survival mode and it was failing. I went and sat in a shop doorway in the Bridges shopping centre. The ground was cold and wet, it didn't matter, I was already soaked through. I sat leaning against the doorway of the shop, in the cold, dark, silent night. My head in my hands I wondered how the hell I had got to this point. Desolate, nowhere to turn, insignificant. I'd spiralled so fast and didn't know how to get out of the pit of despair I had fallen in to. I felt worthless so I began drinking again, it was the only comfort I had.

I got a bed in the hostel. It was an awful place that thankfully has now closed down. People were violent, stole from each other, exploited the vulnerable and death on site was a common occurrence. I had been there a short time when one day, some of us were watching football in the communal lounge. We were all drinking and at this point, my alcoholism was out of control, but it was my reliable friend, my only source of comfort and a way to mute the sounds of failure blaring in my head. I commented on a shot and got verbal abuse from someone. I asked what the problem was and a few of them 'jumped' on me. I was assaulted with an iron bar, kicked and punched. They cut my face to the bone, I have a permanent scar above my lip. They broke my arm and ribs and left me for dead, in the hallway of the hostel. All from a comment about football.

I woke up in the hospital and was discharged quickly in the early morning. I still felt concussed, covered in bandages and my arm in a cast. A police car pulled up and took me to the hostel. I slept for a few days solid. The people who assaulted me never got charged and I hid from them while I recovered and tried to think of how I could get out. It was hard, my mind wasn't my own as alcoholism gripped me. However, one day I saw him coming up the stairs, the main perpetrator who assaulted me within an inch of my life. He didn't see me and I jumped out, kicked him hard in the stomach and he went falling down the stairs. I ran into my tiny room, grabbed my little belongings and fled.

I hadn't thought about where I would go, but I had stood up for myself and this felt like the fuel my soul needed. It wasn't in my nature, but I had to make a stand. This was their lifestyle; assaulting people, violence, bullying, criminality. It wasn't me and I would die if I stayed in this environment, so off I went.

I ran to the bus station, and asked someone which bus was leaving next. It was a bus to Newcastle, so I jumped on it with my small bag of belongings, saying a very happy goodbye to Sunderland. After arriving in Newcastle, I went to the council homeless offices and I was placed in a hostel, which also broke down and I ended up sofa surfing again for a while, bouncing around, self-medicating with alcohol.

Alcohol had its firm hold on me and I was consuming a bottle of spirits a day at this stage. Sobriety almost didn't exist as I kept topping myself up, determined to dull the pain and feelings of failure that pulsed with my heartbeat. I knew I was killing myself and I didn't care. Part of me wanted it, for the shit show to end. I was unrecognisable from the aircraft weapon technician I used to be. The man who had served the country, who took pride in being in the RAF and position. He had gone, there wasn't a trace of him left. Not one part, lingering in the background, keeping everything together. I felt defeated, I'd given up and it was just a matter of time before I could die.

I was 36 years old at this point and weighed around six stone. One morning I came downstairs and knew death was coming, creeping up on me, a sinister shadow. I rang an ambulance and I was admitted to ICU. A few days later, I came out of intensive care but remained hooked up to drips and machines. The doctor told me I was seriously ill. I knew I was and had been for a long time, but to hear it from a medical professional was something else. A finality.

I asked him to clarify and he told me I was going to die. I queried how long I had left and he said I may not make it until the end of the week.

"What day is it?" I asked.

"Tuesday." he said.

"So will I die on Friday or Saturday?" I asked. It was important to me.

"Why, do you have something planned?" the doctor asked.

"Well, you never know," I said in a joking way.

But at that moment, I knew I wasn't ready to die. I didn't want to die. After thinking life was pointless and painful and I was worthless. When it came down to it, I wanted to live!

Three weeks later, I crawled out of the hospital. When I had gone in, my body was shutting down. I was bleeding internally, I had hepatitis, my liver, spleen and kidneys weren't functioning. My body was giving up but my flame of determination was fuelled and I got better. I had a long way to go, physically and mentally, but I left the hospital, sober. Without the drink, I had to face the shame of what I had become. The light had gone on in a previous dark place and I couldn't hide from reality anymore.

I swapped alcohol for education and I began an IT course

in Newcastle, through The Princes Trust. It kept me focused and planted a seed of self-esteem, which I fed and watered and felt it grow. I completed the course, asking to do more and I found the old me slowly returning. I visited the training centre every day and devoured the IT courses, they became my new addiction. One day, I was told a member of staff was going to be off suddenly for a few weeks. They asked if I could help out with teaching. My eyes almost popped out of my head as I answered,

"I'm a fucking alcoholic."

They laughed, said I was good with people and they wanted me to help. I was dumbfounded, someone saw something in me that they used to see in the RAF. A purpose, skills and knowledge. I hadn't felt wanted and appreciated for my skills in so long. Eventually, they convinced me to help and the self-esteem inside me got bigger. I developed my skills and confidence by running the course and helping others. It helped me to stop focusing on my own inadequacies, guilt and problems. The Princes Trust then offered me a teacher training course and after some convincing, I signed up. After a few weeks, I told them I didn't deserve to be there, I felt like a charlatan and my imposter syndrome was suffocating me. I was still an alcoholic and felt like a failure amongst normal, decent people. I had done some terrible things and had lived in amongst some very bad people. They convinced me to stay and the self-esteem began growing again.

I completed the course and I was offered a job with The Princes Trust. It felt like I had found a purpose at last. A focus that helped others as much as it helped me. My life blossomed, I qualified as a teacher in adult education with a Cert ED, worked up to level four ICT, completed management and business support courses and finally completed a BA (hons) degree, I had found a new career! Funding ended however and I spent the next few years working between substance misuse recovery services and training and education. My last post of teaching ended when I was 55 years old and I was made redundant. I began applying for jobs and even with lots of experience and qualifications I wasn't getting any response. It felt hopeless and I needed a solution.

Whilst applying for several jobs and being met with silence, I began thinking about setting up my own service, to support veterans. Operation Veteran became an idea that wouldn't go away, first thing in the morning and last thing at night, it would bounce around in my mind. All the potential, all the people it could support. I began trying to generate interest and raise funds. I was getting nowhere and people didn't seem to be interested. I was determined, so began selling antiques to raise funds and the money was used to start a monthly breakfast club. This is when I met Gary Bell, he helped generate interest as the Armed Forces champion for North Tyneside Council at the time. Veterans started attending and I continued to self-fund the project, for three years, using savings and buying and selling antiques on a local market stall.

I needed published accounts to show we could do it and allow me to apply for funding. As time went on, the more I knew the project was needed. It wasn't just for the local veterans who needed company, help and support, but for me also. The breakfast club, talking to the veterans, it felt natural to me and it was where I belonged.

Those three years were hard. I walked everywhere as I couldn't afford petrol. I remember one day, about three years ago, I had holes in my only pair of shoes. I saved up for three weeks to buy a £20 pair of shoes, making do with wet socks and sore feet until I had that money. To this day, I am always

Me, selling antiques at a local market to raise fund for Operation Veteran

eternally grateful for anything I have and everything we get for the project.

The breakfast club continued to thrive and Gary helped us. We were donated £690 from Darcey's Candles in Scotland, by a wonderful lady and now friend, Jackie Dalziel. This helped us to run the breakfast club twice a month and coffee mornings once a month. Avondale House in Byker then asked us to do a breakfast club and games night there. Everything was going great and I loved it, connecting with the veterans, having a laugh and talking military banter.

By the end of 2019 we were doing really well so I decided to set out a plan for the next year. Then covid hit and the world stopped. I felt back to square one, no money was coming in and I wasn't entitled to any benefits or furlough payments. The chair of North Tyneside council at the time Cllr Wendy Lott, chose Operation Veteran as a charity to support, this was our lifeboat. I began walking the streets, looking for a building. I found a building in North Shields that could be a possibility. It was very run down, electrics were broken and it was in a state of disrepair. Despite this, it had potential. I only had a small amount of money from the council and the rent was significantly more over the year. I could walk away or I could make it work. Of course, I decided on the latter and took on the building, with all its magnolia walls, dirty carpets and radiators hanging off the wall. It needed a lot of love and attention. I set about a plan, to get the centre safe, colourful, welcoming and comfortable on a shoe-string budget. Word got out and soon we had offers of help from local people, who had an affinity with the forces. Some had served themselves, or their parents or children had. Local veterans came and helped out moving items, decorating, reno-vating and collecting donations. We all mucked in and the old camaraderie felt like a warm blanket on the chilliest of days. I felt so proud, so grateful and Operation Veteran HQ was offi-cially born.

Operation Veteran HQ. Me, second from left

We did what we could in lockdown, monthly beach walks that became so popular they ended up weekly. As things eased we opened, socially distancing and used our backyard. Normality returned and we were able to offer the services we wanted to; a drop-in, a place for food, company and chats. Somewhere you'll always find a friendly face and advice if you need it, a community. The main focus is everything we do and all services we offer for veterans are free. We have a café on site that is open to anyone and upstairs we have our drop-in and some of our activities. We are a small, brilliant team and are securing funding each year. We have had help from Toni at The Business Factory and belief from so many funders as well as the community.

It doesn't feel like work, it feels like my life and I'm grateful for life every single day!

Me, right, Operation Veteran – Queen Elizabeth II memorial (Sept 2022)

Dedicated to everyone involved in Operation Veteran.

Her Majesty's Territorial Army
John Aitchison

Name: John Aitchison
Age: 69 years old
Armed Forces, Regiment / Rank: Territorial Army (TA), Royal Engineers, 72 Engineer Regiment, 103 Squadron, SAPPER
Date entered: May 1970
Date left: Jan 2013

At the age of 17, I joined the TA. It was 1970 and I began my TA career at Heaton barracks, Newcastle, being recruited as a SAPPER in the Royal Engineers. My father had been in the British Army, serving in the Royal Army Service Corps as a chef, during WWII. He built an oven in the war that was given the title of 'Geordie's oven,' built from what he could scavenge in order to feed himself and his comrades. After the war, my father went on to work as a baker all his life.

I first joined the TA after being influenced by a friend who was serving. He would talk about the TA, as a big adventure and a way to learn new skills. It sounded great and that positive impression and decision of action was the start of my 43 years in the TA. After joining, I began recruit training, resulting in a recruits course at Cove, Hampshire. We travelled down in our army uniform, via London and after a long train journey we eventually arrived. The training was great fun and after completion, I went on to learn the various modules involved in trade training for the Engineers.

In those days there were many tall, strong lads in the Engineers, mainly coming from heavy industry work and there was me, a short, 8 ½ stone, young lad. What I lacked compared to the others in weight and height, I more than made up for in enthusiasm. However, lifting the huge, weighty girders was impossible for me, so I was assigned the running-around jobs. I would be the pin man when we built bridges and would use the Cowley level, which would assist with transfer elevations during construction. It suited me fine and I enjoyed the tasks and being part of the team. At the time, we used to build Medium Girder and Bailey bridges. There were several aspects to the role of a field engineer; building bridges, watermanship and demolitions. Our regiment trained all around the North including Northumberland, Yorkshire and Cumbria.

In my engineering days, we had some amazing times. I passed my driving test, learnt new skills such as signalling and enjoyed all aspects of the role. I joined the recruiting team at my squadron, training new recruits in the way of the military. Once my regiment learnt that I could read and write I was tasked with completing the admin for new recruits. This lead me to becoming chief clerk, as admin was always my main thrust.

There were three squadrons within the regiment and one year we were assigned the job of building a youth hostel in Scotland.

Army recruit training, Hampshire (1970) Me: First row, first left.

The three squadrons all played their part; the first going for two weeks to lay the foundations of the building. Next was my squadron, who built the structure for two weeks and finally, the third squadron for the final two weeks completed the building. We would take on tasks, supporting the local government to build structures. This included bridges and on one occasion building ladders for salmon to travel up. During this time, the lads were in the river, capturing the fish. We ended up eating 2olb salmon each night for dinner! A change in role came when we were nominated to become a Harrier support squadron. The Engineers were asked to lay landing pads and runways and build the hides for the harriers. This was hard and tedious labour. Luckily, I didn't have to do it as I was in the signals section at the time, but the squadron had to and complained as it was extremely hard work, having to secure the pads and runways with three foot pickets. The one consolation was that we were eating with the RAF and the food was superb.

The camps with the Engineers were always interesting. My first camp after completing my recruits course was to Hamlin, Germany and it was a real eye-opener. At the time, it was the Cold War period and we were tasked with preparing demolitions over bridges. This was needed as if we were to go to war with the Russians, each unit within the British Army had a certain area to cover and we would have ended up there, blowing up bridges and retreating, trying to stop the enemy from advancing. Another year, we went to Belgium where we were required to move a commemorative monument of the light infantry from a hill that people tended not to visit. We did this as a regimental task, completing everything within the six week timeframe. When they were digging the foundations, rounds and weapon parts were discovered, 25 years after the Second World War. Also during this camp, we visited Passchendaele and Tyne Cot Cemetery, which is a burial ground of WWI soldiers. Tyne Cot is the largest cemetery for Commonwealth forces in the world for any war and has thousands of unnamed graves.

Alongside being in the TA, at the time, I worked at Rowntrees Ltd and enjoyed life as a civilian. In 1971, when I was 18 years old, I met my wife-to-be, Sheila. We met in the Queen Alexandra pub in North Shields and married in 1976.

By 1979, I was a staff sergeant in the Engineers and I was appointed Squadron Chief Clerk. Then by around 1983, it began to become less appealing. I wasn't impressed with the management structure or the surrounding politics and felt it was time for a new challenge. I was at a crossroads, where I was ready to leave unless I was tempted by another opportunity. One of the pay clerks suggested moving to the Royal Artillery and thinking I had nothing to lose, I decided I would give it a try. It was a massive change in direction. I would work the guns now and then and spend time on the command post, but the majority of the role was admin. I reverted back to sergeant as there was already a staff sergeant. So I transferred to 101 Regiment Royal Artillery and I was posted to South Shields, at 205 Battery. The team there were great and the recruiter was Peter Thomas, who became a lifelong friend. In the Artillery, the main focus was firing and supporting the Guns. We attended a few large exercises in Germany and I remember one exercise, there were several units up at Albemarle Barracks in Ouston. There were TA units from all over and once we left there was a convoy of vehicles that was 12 miles long going to the port in North Shields, bound for Germany. It was incredible.

One year, whilst travelling to camp in Germany, the regiment disembarked from the ferry in Holland. All of the vehicles drove off and turned left, except for one Gun who turned right and ended up lost, driving towards France for four days with very limited supplies. When they finally found us, they were tired and hungry, eventually finding the funny side as we mocked them all day, and for months afterwards! I also remember during camp in Germany, everyone enjoyed drinking Apfelkorn. For the newer lads, they were drinking it like pop and there were a lot of bad heads on many mornings.

Over the years I attended some very interesting and enjoyable camps. I visited North Carolina and Michigan attached to the US National Guard. I went on an amazing battlefield tour to South Africa. I also travelled to Germany on several occasions, as well as Belgian, Holland and Lithuania and went to camps all over the UK.

Woolwich Barracks (Nov, 1987) Me, second row, fifth from left.

During two instances I was acting as a terrorist, travelling around the Home Counties and being watched by the Intelligence Corps eventually being picked up in the early morning by the police and interrogated.

I was promoted to Warrant Officer Class 2 in 1987 and remained at 205 Battery in South Shields until 1992. As my role was predominately administering and training recruits, Young lads would come in, many full of enthusiasm and could have made good soldiers, but their literacy skills were abysmal. It seemed a travesty that 18-year-olds were coming through the door without the ability to read and write, in the 80s and 90s. Our team would process the new recruits, from the start of the enlistment process until passing out as trained soldiers. Over the years, I would estimate I was involved in recruiting 2,500-3,000 recruits and in between recruitment, we would go to camp and help out with other tasks.

Throughout my time in the TA, I probably enjoyed the recruitment side of it the most. It was wonderful to see a lad come through the door, apprehensive, timid and sometimes almost frightened of their own shadow. Only to leave, four months later after completing their training and passing out, two feet taller. Maybe not in physique but definitely in confidence. Even if they didn't go on to be a soldier, it was magical to see; lads being set for life with pride, respect, confidence and direction alongside experiencing the camaraderie the military offered. To this day, I sometimes see (not so young) lads who remember me from their training days and say "Hello." It is great and it is what we were all about at the TA.

In 2004, I was honoured to receive the Queen's Voluntary Reservists Medal (QVRM). It was a memorable day at Buckingham Palace and a privilege to be recognised for my contribution in the TA. It was something I was really proud of, as there are only 13 awarded each year throughout all the reserve forces. I was also nominated for an MBE by a colleague in 1993, which was a magnificent honour, even though I didn't receive the appointment.

Receiving my QVRM from Queen Elizabeth II (2004)

An opportunity arose within recruiting in 2004, when the brigade decided to create recruiting teams and divide them into north and south areas. I applied for the north role and was successful being in charge of a team of six from various units. I was given two vehicles, a recruiting trailer and a climbing wall. Myself and the team would go all over; to events, fairs and shopping centres, across the North East. The climbing wall got most of the attention, with the kids loving it, but having all of the recruiting literature, it was good PR and we could speak and share information with people who wanted more than to climb up the wall. I continued in this role for around four years, then the bookings slowed down and it was becoming tiring being a children's activity entertainer when the wall came out!

Sheila and I, Buckingham Palace (2004)

The social side of the TA was also brilliant. When I was younger it was a drinking club and there used to be some heavy sessions in the bar. There were many dinners and functions that spouses could attend and my wife, Sheila and I enjoyed many social events. Sheila made friends with colleague's wives and the whole family could be included in events at times such as Christmas parties. By the time I was 30 years old, I had drunk as much as I wanted to drink, through the TA! There isn't an open drinking culture now in the TA and the Cadets, times have changed and this feels like a positive change.

When I first joined the TA, you had to retire at 45 years old. As time went on, this was extended to 55 years old. I was very fortunate and asked to stay on, remaining until I was 60 years old. By this time, the TA had come a very long way from the drinking club it was when I joined in 1970.

Me, left, being presented with a Commandants Coin for service to Durham Army Cadet Force, annual camp (2022). Presented by Colonel NW Foster, Commandant Durham Army Cadet Force.

I became involved with the Cadets 15 years ago after the retired colonel of 101 Regiment became involved with Durham Cadets and asked for my assistance with the admin. Each year, I supported the camp and when I was 65 years old, I was given a year's extension. Then when I was scheduled to sign on again I was told I couldn't, given my age. However, the process changed due to not being able to age discriminate and I am still working there now. I attend annual camps working in county headquarters supporting admin processes. I received a long service Cadet medal for 12 years' service in 2019. It was wonderful to receive it for something I enjoy doing.

Throughout my time in the TA, I worked a further job as a civilian. After working at Rowntrees Ltd, I secured employment at Proctor & Gamble and Eventcover Productions, in various admin and management roles. Sheila and I went on to have two daughters, Joanne, now 44 years old and Helen, now 41 years old and we have a phenomenal, beautiful grand-daughter, Elise.

After leaving the TA in 2013, I continued to work full-time as a runner/artist liaison in the music industry. This involved supporting local music and entertainment venues such as The City Hall, Tyne Theatre, O2 Academy and The Sage, providing assistance to visiting musicians, singers, bands and cultural figures. It was diverse and enjoyable. I met some great famous people, many of who were very down to earth, despite their fame. I remember being the runner for Alice Cooper. He was a brilliant guy and asked me why women in Newcastle never wore coats on nights out (something the Geordie women are known for)! I turn 70 years old at the end of this year, but I still work most days. I work event security and front of house for local events and culture organisations such as The Sage, Gateshead and The Theatre Royal,

Newcastle. It keeps me busy and helps pay for the many holiday's Sheila and I like to enjoy each year.

The military isn't for everyone, but for many, it can be the stepping stone to their best life. I would say there is nothing to lose by trying it and possibly everything to gain. I spent more than half of my life in the TA and it shaped me as a young lad and as an adult. I enjoyed it all and luckily, still have friends from my time in the TA. Being involved in the Cadets continues my service in a small way and I will remain supporting the yearly camps for as long as I can.

Dedicated to my wife Sheila and daughters, Joanne and Helen.

Forever Thankful
John Edward Knowles

Name: John Edward Knowles
Age: 80 years old
Armed Forces, Regiment / Rank: British Army, Royal Army Medical Corps, WO2 RQMS
Tours / Conflicts served: Malaya, Berlin, Cyprus, Rinteln, UK
Date entered: February 1958
Date left: December 1981

I was born in December 1941 in Norfolk and named John. This was to honour my father's favourite brother who had recently died from pneumonia after having a tooth out and cycling home in freezing weather. Edward was chosen as my middle name, continuing a family tradition as this was also my father's and my great uncle's middle name. My great uncle was killed in the great war and his name is on the war memorial in Holt, Norfolk, along with my own name.

I was educated at the local primary school, then having passed my 11+ went to the City of Norwich Grammar

School for the first two years of my secondary education. In 1954 my father was promoted from his job at Eastern Counties Omnibus Company and became the Manager at the Kings Lynn depot. We all moved to a new house in West Lynn, and I was then sent to the King Edward 7th grammar school in Kings Lynn. I hated every minute of it and eventually left the school aged 15 in 1957. After leaving school I worked on the ferry boat that carried passengers between West Lynn and Kings Lynn for a few months, upping my hours to full-time after previously working there in holidays and some weekends. I would often spend Sundays on the ferry boat sailing into the The Wash and fishing for plaice which we sold to the local fish & chip shop.

I had already been to the recruiting office to enquire about joining the RAMC Army Apprentices College. With the blessing of my parents, I signed on the dotted line, eager to begin a new adventure, see the world and learn a trade. On February 11th, 1958, a skinny, 5'2", 16-year-old who looked about 11 years old, disembarked the train at Fleet Station and boarded a 3-ton truck for the journey to Queen Elizabeth Barracks, Church Crookham, Hampshire. This was the beginning of a 23-year career with the Royal Army Medical Corps.

For the next 1¾ years I completed my training, which included basic training, education and my specialist trade training. It was intense, in a whole new environment but I passed, obtaining my qualifications and learning things about myself and life lessons in the process. I made many friends, who all had a backstory to tell and went on to have their own, unique stories of military life. I met one apprentice, training at the same time as myself, at a RAMC Association branch meeting in Norwich 40 years later, to discover we lived close to one another. All those years passed, but memories remain strong and the camaraderie of the forces means the connection and laughs never fade.

RAMC Apprentices College, Church Crookham
(1958). Me, front row, second from left

My next posting was BMH Catterick for a year or so, before being sent on detachment to MRS Ranby Camp, near Retford. This unit was a RASC Tank Transporter Company and I was there for a few months. After Retford, I was posted to Milbank, in my opinion the finest Military Hospital the British Army has ever known. Whilst stationed at Milbank, I participated in the Turning of the Pages Ceremony at Westminster Abbey in February 1963.

Also during my time here, I met my wife to be, Babs, at the Nuffield Centre just off Trafalgar Square. After a wonderful period of courting, we married in March 1963.We moved into a top-floor flat in Ealing and our first daughter, Brenda, was born in January 1964.

I qualified as an NO 1 (Nursing Orderly First Class) and was then sent on detachment to Windsor with the Household Cavalry. I met some characters during this time, in particular my superior, surgeon lieutenant colonel. His mode of transport was an old London Taxi and to ensure soldiers were not late for duty, he would wait at the train station in Windsor, offering a lift but charging the soldier's a small fee. If the soldier declined his offer and was subsequently late for duty, he made sure that a 252 charge sheet was raised. On another occasion, he referred a horse to Milbank for an ECG! One day on sick parade, I was in the MO's office assisting the surgeon lieutenant colonel, when a soldier came in with an obscure illness. The lieutenant colonel duly examined him, before advising him to kneel down and repeat "Dear Lord, please help me as the Doctor can do nothing for me."

In May 1964 I was posted to 16 Commonwealth Field Ambulance, Terendak Camp Malacca, Malaya. I was going to a country I knew virtually nothing about, not even where it was! Malaysia has since become the country outside of England that we love the most. We worked hard and played hard with Babs joining me about three months into my posting. As a family, we lived in private accommodation outside of camp for about a year, before being allocated married quarters on camp. It was absolute paradise, with swimming pools, a glorious tropical beach and house staff. A life of luxury for three years and like something out of the movies.

A memorable moment occurred about two weeks after arriving in Malaysia. There was an alert and I was issued with an SMG with 28 rounds of ammo and told to guard a section of the camp. Usually, RAMC did not routinely carry weapons, but it was all available called to be on guard duty. At about 3 am, I heard a noise in the jungle. I called "Halt, who goes there?" to an echo of silence. A minute later the noise began again. Once more I called out, releasing the safety catch on my weapon. I was about to pull the trigger when a huge water buffalo came trotting towards me. This big, noisy beast was in its own stomping ground, probably wondering what the hell I was doing. I then knew what adrenaline smelt like!

When in the jungle of Malaya, you had to make do with what tools and equipment you had. Of course, the brain was often your biggest tool and all the training you had absorbed. One time we were training in the jungle when a New Zealander slipped and broke his ankle. With the limited first aid supplies available I strapped it up and tried to arrange the making of a stretcher to carry him out. The New Zealander's section sergeant asked us all to give up one of our two water bottles, which he tied to the injured soldier, then gently manoeuvred him into the nearby river where he floated downstream to the nearest road. It took several hours before he was met by a land rover ambulance and taken to Terendak hospital. When we were in Malaya for the Merdeka celebrations in 2007 I met up with some New Zealanders from the same regiment as the injured soldier. They remembered the incident and we smiled, talking about teamwork. Sadly, he had passed away some years earlier.

Me, carrying a casualty out of the jungle, Malaya (1964)
Public relations photo. Now in IWM Collection

Another wonderful memory I have is from being on duty in the Families Medical Centre. I was woken by a soldier in the early hours asking me to do a 'home visit' as his wife had very severe abdominal pain. I went to the house with him, ready to treat his wife and a few minutes later delivered a bouncing baby girl.

In mid-1965, I was sent as lance corporal, on unaccompanied detachment to OP Crown, an airfield being constructed in North East Thailand. We were told the airfield was being constructed to improve communications in Thailand. Perhaps a pure coincidence that the Vietnam War was in its infancy. We were within a stone's throw of the Lao border and the Americans had a radar station only a couple of miles away from us. The big advantage of being so close to the Americans was that they had fresh milk parachuted in two or three times a week along with their other rations. They always had a surplus and those of us in the Medical Centre managed to claim the leftovers on many occasions. As an added bonus, they gave us the choice of Strawberry or Chocolate flavoured milk! This detachment was probably the most memorable of my career and I know it was for many others who served there. As Medics, we treat hundreds of locals, with some having walked for days to get treatment from us. We were told that the average local family would have ten children in the hope that three would mature. TB was everywhere, diarrhoea was commonplace and there were virtually no antibiotics available to the locals, except from us. The nearest local hospital was 50 miles away in Ubon, Ratchathani.

I remember a middle-aged, male patient who had been bitten on the foot by a cobra. His friend immediately took out a machete, and chopped part of his foot off! We treated him throughout my tour there and eventually, the REME Workshops made him a 'peg leg.' On another occasion I was honoured by a local family to help light the funeral pyre for their father who had passed away. The team worked hard in Thailand and it made a difference to the local people, it was literally their lifeline. I have many happy memories of this time and it was the only place that I had served where Babs and I had not returned to since leaving the Corps, until 2010, when we finally returned on a reunion. It was a great occasion, with a trip down memory lane for so many of us. Sadly the village had changed a lot but our group were 'guests of honour' at the Remembrance Day Service in Ubon and I was asked to lay a wreath on behalf of the Op Crown Association. It was an honour and I am delighted we got to return. After my stint in Thailand, I returned to Malaya, back to my Babs and our children. Our second daughter, Carol, was born in April 1965 followed by our son, John, in July 1966. We then decided to hire a television as we realised what was causing the babies to keep appearing!

My next posting was BMH Berlin, by which point I had been promoted to corporal. Initially, the hospital was in Radalandstrase, in the Spandau suburbs, then in 1967 we moved to a brand new purpose-built hospital in Charlottenburg. The second floor of the building was designed to house Rudolf Hess as a patient, if necessary. This did become necessary during my time there. When Hess became a patient, it was my job to escort the Soviet doctor and interpreter on their daily visit. For the three weeks or so that Hess was a patient, the doctor only ever spoke to me through the interpreter. However, on his last visit it was a particularly cold, wet windy day. We were going to the ward in the lift and the Doctor turned round to me, smiled and said in perfect English, "Bloody cold today, isn't it!" Berlin was a fascinating city to live in, especially in the 60s with the Cold War at its height.

In late 1969, another posting came through to Mytchett House, Keogh, as a unit first aid instructor. It was a coincidence that Rudolf Hess was kept as a Prisoner of War in Mytchett House for most of his time in captivity. I did not really enjoy my time there and after six months managed to be appointed as a recruiting sergeant in sunny Bournemouth.

From there we were posted to even sunnier Cyprus. A fantastic place to live, with the working day finishing at lunchtime and sporting activities top of the list for leisure time. I was a member of the Karting Club and also managed to gain my glider pilot's licence, but sadly had to stop flying after my three solo flights as the Turks decided to invade the island. This was an interesting time, with refugees fleeing into the sovereign base area and the phantom bombers of the Turkish Air Force flying quite close to our borders. A memorable time was when the Royal Navy helicopter from HMS Hermes flew in an underslung load of Turkish sailors that had been in the water for about a week. The story behind this, was that a Turkish warship, the Kocatepe, was approaching Kyrenia in Northern Cyprus in 'disguise' as a Greek ship. When the Turkish Air Force saw the ship, they immediately bombed it, causing it to sink with all on board. A day or so later, I was tasked to deliver these unfortunate souls to the Turkish authorities for burial in temporary graves in occupied territory. A British military vehicle had been mistakenly attacked a day before. So I decided to escort the truck with the bodies on board in my own car, having loaned a union jack from the stores, I draped this over the top of my car and drove 100 yards in front of the truck. My heart was in my mouth during that journey but it went without incident.

One unusual task I was volunteered for, by the hospital gynaecologist, was to cater for HRH Princess Margaret on her visit to the hospital. My role was to open the car door for her on arrival at the hospital, hold her cigarettes and lighter, serve her a brandy sour and a couple of G & T's. Then my remit included standing behind her chair at lunch, whilst she and the other VIP's ate and my stomach rumbled. The best part was that when HRH arrived, she handed me a bouquet that had been presented to her at her previous location. Not everyone can say that royalty has given them flowers! They took pride of place in my lounge at home for a while and made Babs and I smile like a child at a funfair each time we passed them.

From Cyprus, it was to Rinteln for three years. I had been promoted to staff sergeant and enjoyed my posting. The hospital was on the outskirts of a beautiful German town, with very friendly locals and a huge catchment area. From Rinteln, I was sent to 219 Wx General Hospital, a TA Unit in Keynsham, where I became a warrant officer class 2 (RQMS). My PSO was Major Roger Nutbeem, one of the best bosses I had known throughout my service. He had a married quarter in the same close as Babs and I, not only was he my boss, but he also became a very good friend. Sadly, he was killed in action in the Falklands when his unit was on the Sir Galahad. A great loss to the Corps, his family and his many friends. I left Keynsham in mid-1981 to spend around six months left of my army career with a TA unit only about 500 yards from where I was born in Mile Cross, Norwich. I was finishing where the seed for my whole career was planted, at home in Norwich.

On discharge in December 1981, I was employed for my first 20 months as a civilian with Securicor. The BUPA Hospital was being built in Norwich and I was fortunate enough to obtain a job as the store manager, spending almost 20 years with BUPA before being made redundant, some nine months after I should have retired!

Babs and I, Buckingham Palace (2015)

Since retiring we have had the most enjoyable times ever. Life has been so kind to us both. We have been to Royal Garden Parties at Buckingham Palace and a reception at Sandringham with the late Queen Elizabeth II. In 2007, we travelled to Malaysia and I was awarded the PJM Medal by the Malaysian Deputy Prime Minister. After the medal presentation in Kuala Lumpur, with around 42 other veterans, I took part in a parade with 24,600 others through the streets of Kuala Lumpur. This was one of the highlights of a fantastic life and after the parade we met the then, HRH Prince Andrew at a reception in the Ambassador's Residence. For several years now I have also been a member of the RAMC Association, the Royal Norfolk Veterans Association and the National Malaya and Borneo Veterans Association. I have been honoured to carry the RAMC Association Branch Standard for several parades and on three occasions to carry it at the Turning of the Pages Ceremony at Westminster Abbey, and also carried the Union Standard for the NMBVA at a service in St Pauls Cathedral, London.

Receiving my PJM medal from the Malaysian Deputy
PM, Kuala Lumpur (2007)

My retirement job for a few years, was with a local under-
taker, driving and bearing on funerals. This helped us to enjoy
life and have many holidays in our later lives. Sadly, we have
both lost family members and friends as the years have passed.
But we have always had each other.

We moved to Northumberland in 2011 to be closer to our
eldest daughter, our son and two grandchildren. Since being
here I have had health problems; my mobility and ongoing
issues with my heart. I have an abdominal aortic aneurysm
that I am due an operation for. However, we keep as fit as we
can and attend the Operation Veteran weekly walks as well as
the drop-in now and then. It is a great place, with a wonderful
bunch of people and we have both made friends for life. I am
a member of the local branch of the RAMC Association and
Babs and I are part of the local branch of the National Malaya
and Borneo Veterans Association. We also joined a local lawn
bowls club and spend many hours practicing, playing and
even competing with lovely friends.

Babs and I have been the best of friends and soul mates all

At Westminster Abbey, carrying the RAMC Standard (2005)

our lives. I am grateful for so many precious memories that we continue to make to this day. I can say with all honesty, that with thanks to the Corps and of course the support and love of my dear Babs, I have had possibly the most enjoyable life that anyone could wish for. I will be forever thankful for what the RAMC has done for me. I would never change a thing; there have been far more ups than downs. What would I have done, since February 1958 and where would I be now, if it had not been for the RAMC and of course Babs?

Dedicated to my wife, Babs Knowles, who has been by my side for the past 60 years. Also to all those comrades who have gone on their final posting, joining other veterans who served our wonderful country.

Digging In With Your Eyelids
Mark Graham (née Harle) Golderharle

Name: Mark Graham (née Harle) Golderharle
Age: 37 years old
Armed Forces, Regiment / Rank: British Army Royal Corp of Signals; Served in 3 (UK) Division Signal Regiment, 22 Signal Regiment, 1 (UK) Armored Division Signal Regiment. Sergeant.
Tours / Conflicts served: Two tours of Afghanistan – Op Herrick 11 (2009/2010), Op Herrick 15/16 (2011/2012).
Date entered: December 2001
Date left: Sept 2012

I joined the army in December 2001, having just turned 17 years old. My family did not want me to join the army as frontline infantry. My father's partner had a relative who was in the Royal Signals and this became an appealing option and would mean I would join and gain a trade.

Being under 18 years old, I could enter the army, meaning I would join a college apprenticeship and my chosen role would be as a system engineer technician. Although I committed to joining in August 2001, and swore my Oath of Allegiance in December 2001, I could not start the apprenticeship until the next intake in January 2002. So after my GCSE's in the Summer of 2001, even though I was keen to join the military, My dad did the 'parent thing' of not allowing me to doss about for six months and encouraged me to sign up to sixth form college, albeit that it may only be for a short time.

Here I continued my studies until the apprenticeship commenced within the army, studying advanced mathematics and computer sciences, which would propel me in my technician role in the military. Alongside my studies, I was able to participate in my second love, rugby. I played locally with Percy Park and participated in skills training with Newcastle Falcons, with the likes of Johnny Wilkinson and alongside fellow players such as Toby Flood. It was a big part of my life that sadly ended, for the most part, when I joined the army.

I left home in January 2002 for phase one training at Arborfield, near Reading. I felt ten feet tall as we were told we were the 'leaders of the future,' commencing our eight-month training, which included educational qualifications. The training was intense and an emotional experience as a young person adjusting to a new environment. Getting shouted at was a constant, ear-offending chime. We had to march everywhere we went and if it wasn't strong, bold, perfect, a voice would blare at us.

To add offence to the verbal insults, there were no home comforts on the camp. The beds were metal, small and uncomfortable. Luxury was a thing of the past. The doctrine felt old-fashioned and some of the furniture could have been from the Second World War also. We were always on duty and alongside this regimented training and deconstruction of our former selves, we had the studying. All the preparation we needed to go to war. I recall being exhausted all of the time, physically and mentally. It felt like a marathon of endurance. The level of study, assessment detail and grueling exercises seemed to never end.

It was of course, the way to change us, from civilians to soldiers. Strip us of our lives before and train us to be defending and killing machines before being individuals. I remember in our induction, we were given haircuts. We all went in, waiting for our trim but there was no barber banter of holidays or even a 'what would you like today?' Instead, we were all given the same, short shave, watching as part of our identity fluttered to the floor.

Some people didn't survive beyond a few weeks of basic training. We were all young, but the army meant business and if you didn't conform, or if you showed any sign of struggle, you were out. For those of us who did make it, we became like a family. We would get reports, on our conduct, learning and behavior. There was a girl that I met at camp, Krystle. We became close and had a relationship. It was all quite innocent and we were good support for one another.

We got paid weekly, cash at first and we would spend all of our wages each weekend on junk food! There was little else to do and our fellow trainees were the only company we knew. Eventually, we had to open a bank account and I remember the day we were marched to the bank, chosen by the army. Another push through the 'sausage factory.'

On completion of basic training and to progress to trade training (phase two), we moved on to Blandford, in Dorset. Krystle had an injury, so was held back, as was our relationship. After a year of trade training, I moved to my first working unit. Around six months later, I found out that Krystle had taken her own life by hanging. I was still very young, as was Krystle when she died and it was my first real experience of losing someone. The pain felt even more brutal given her age and someone I was so close to. All the thoughts of the things she would never be able to do and feelings of sadness for a wasted life. It felt too difficult to comprehend. I reflected as I got older and I still think of Krystle. At the time, we were so young and the army was reducing us to very basic humans. It is their job in many ways but there was not the emotional support. You couldn't ask for help so you simply didn't ask for help. We were programmed, regimented, dehumanized. Then something would happen and reality, or lack of our normal reality, would hit like a cannonball, pulling apart the scaffolding that was being built around you. The scaffolding used to change parts of you.

Alongside this and the building of a new 'you,' there was the survival of the fittest mentality and the competition, often ruthless competition. There was bullying like there is in many institutions and workplaces. I spent a long time thinking about the 'what ifs?' for Krystle. I had a car at the time, what if I would have travelled to see her or should I have called more? Could I have done something? Anything? It haunted me for a long time afterwards and I will never forget Krystle. A tragedy on so many levels.

Training tactics in the army were cold war style, it was harsh, exhausting, pushed us physically and mentally to the limit. Drills, routines, and processes would be repeated, again and again and again like the second hand on a clock, round and round, repeated. But for us, we had to perfect any mistakes, any millimeter of error that could determine life or death.

Trade training at Blandford built my skills as a technician in the Royal Signals, which alongside my role as a soldier first and foremost, would be my specialist trade. Here I learnt a variety of skills, basics such as wiring a plug to massive systems such as Ptarmigan, a 1970s system, designed to provide secure and reliable communications in battle. We would be working on vehicles using noisy generators, covered in camouflaged netting, practicing our skills to ensure communication systems were reliable and lifesaving.

We were all still very young and there was a culture of drinking alcohol, as most of us were just turning 18 years old. We would all go to the same bars in Blandford, which wasn't a massive place, but was booming with all the military folk. In the early 2000s many people didn't have mobile phones, there were limited ways to communicate with family and your comrades were your main family. Drinking and smoking became a massive part of life, for some it created dependencies. Our money was basically 'beer tokens,' that we spent. Some drank out of boredom, some as a stress release and some as escapism. There was something really sad about the ways we wanted to erase the week and sweep away the mind clutter into the bin. It was accepted, expected and the norm.

During my trade training, there was a colleague who became my best buddy. He was from St. Lucia and we were very close. We would attend our days of lectures and studies, then sharing a four or six-man room when the working day was over. We each had our own bed spaces

1 (UK) ADSR in Herford, Germany. Me, middle row, 4th from left.

with dividing walls. There was such limited privacy, we used to pin our issued scratchy blankets on the wall for privacy. We were young lads, we needed our privacy! However, I remember so many of my lunch breaks being spent just getting a quick power nap. The physical and mental training was intense and there was no room for error, which meant concentration levels depleted your energy. We used to say that a good technician was a sleeping technician, indicating that you had completed all your jobs and could rest. With basic training and trade training, we all learnt to sleep anywhere and anytime we could. We also learnt to sleep with our weapons, whilst on exercise, which had to be on us at all times. Like a child with a teddy bear, we kept hold and became comfortable with the uncomfortable.

At the end of trade training, to a degree, you got a choice of units to be posted to. We called the nicer places like Cyprus and some posts in Germany the 'Gucci postings'. I ended up with Bulford, in Wiltshire, which was far less glamourous and appealing for a young lad from North Tyneside. There was little to do in Bulford and by the time Thursday night came around, the serious drinking started for the weekend. Even though we worked on a Friday, there was an unwritten rule that Friday was a half day. Then it would be drinking all weekend with our beer tokens. It's a good job age was on my side! As well as drinking, I enjoyed gaming, so I did have a distraction and something to do other than consuming alcohol. I never went home as it was so far away and a group of us got nicknamed 'The Bulford Orphans.'

Much of our work was greasing and degreasing the Ptarmigan vehicles and looking after the equipment. Our days were mainly spent waiting, practicing and preparing with weeks of exercises. Boredom was a regular thing. When I completed trade training, prior to the posting in 2004, I was given my lance corporal rank. There were times I was advising soldiers in ranks above mine that there were modifications needed on the kit or pointing out something wasn't right. It was hard for some to take from a junior, in years as well as rank. During this first working unit, my staff sergeant was a great guy which really helped. He was inspiring, motivating and showed us respect. I still see he is doing well through the power of social media.

There were some potentially very dangerous times and luck was on my side more times than I had downed a pint of beer. Sometimes all the experience and research, knowledge and experiments do not prepare you for a situation. Human error is always there. I would spend time on high-powered electronics that were outdated and decades old after an intense, condensed training period. Old generators, teleprinters and other electronics with serious voltage running through them. One time I was working on a battery kit at the back of a Land Rover. Instead of a red and black cable connecting them, there were two black cables. I was trying to fix it and after connecting one end the cable started flipping around, sparking. It melted some of my uniform but could have been a lot worse.

By 2006 I was a corporal. In my role, I was effectively a more senior technician but also a soldier, so had to complete my Junior Commanders course. We trained to lead a section of troops, as well as the some of the roles above. I struggled with this course, it was very physical and I had been studying for my trade for so long that my physical side of fitness wasn't always on top form. Although I loved running, it was not as much of a part of my daily life as it was for others. The training was back at Blandford and for me, it brought back all the memories of Krystle. I struggled and it showed. My superiors noticed but I passed, by the skin of my teeth, despite the exhaustion and sleep deprivation they forced on us and my emotions about Krystle.

As a corporal, I had managed to get a temporary assignment to the Falklands. This was my first experience of working with the other branches of the Armed Forces; the

Royal Navy and RAF. There was a radar communication bearer system on the island that we were looking after, with relays on the mountains, manned by the military. One of my main responsibilities was changing the cryptography, for the radio communication between the mountain sites and base. It was more digital by this point, however a ticket tape system that had to be run through a machine at the same time was still needed. The process of going through each site one call one at a time was time-consuming. I decided to change the method, calling all the sites to run the tape through the devices at the same time.

I put my plan into action and then all the island went dark! The computer screen icons began going red or went off. A Navy Commander rang asking where his radar was. Quickly I said it was getting sorted and we had to bring in the Crypto Cell who looked after the tape issuing. It transpired the sites had been given the wrong day's tape. It was believed they had been given the day ahead by mistake. But this was something I enjoyed my job; developing, experimenting where safe to do so and trying to find solutions to processes that were convoluted, outdated and time-consuming. Maybe just not implementing the improvement in the right way at the time!

We had no personal internet in the Falklands and I would go to the local internet café once a day, to use our rationed minutes. We all used websites such as MySpace, Where Are You Now? and 'Hot or Not.' The latter rated people by looks, 1-10. I started talking to a girl in Peru and whilst chatting, she invited me over during my RnR. I had a few weeks leave, had no commitments at home and thought why not! So off I went, travelling to Peru to meet the girl I had been talking to. On my arrival, it turned out she was heavily religious, so I soon learnt nothing intimate was going to happen! I was however, welcomed in by her family and friends. I stayed with her family friend and it was a lovely trip. One of their friends took me around Lima. I played football in the forces and wanted some goal keeper gloves so we went shopping. I noticed lots of people stopping and looking and rushing around me. It turned out that my tour guide had told everyone that I played football for Newcastle United with Nobby Solano, who was a top player for the team at the time. I also got a lot of female attention on the trip as a blonde-haired, blue-eyed young man. Lima was stunning and I saw the most wonderful sites. There was a darker less magical side, in particular children begging, I saw the slum areas and miles of inadequate housing that was situated on the hillsides, above the beach. The people in the slums would come down to serve the tourists and try and sell items. It broke my heart to imagine how difficult their lives were. The divide in the world, things we hear about, know about, but don't always see. I saw it there and it stays with me to this day. The army opened my eyes to these divisions; of poverty to beliefs, motives, agendas and humanity.

After the Falklands and a short posting to MoD Stafford, I spent some time in Herford, Germany. By this time, I had gotten married. My now ex-wife and children moved back, close to where I was posted, a few years after I left the forces. During my time in Germany, I continued progressing in the army, studying and learning my trade.

My next posting was in Kandahar, Afghanistan in 2009/2010. There were rocket attacks from mountains just behind our base, old Chinese rockets that were left from previous conflicts. Weapon caches were still being found. The Taliban would find these rockets and aim them toward the American military. We were taught all the drills but it felt like we were constantly throwing ourselves to the floor, 'digging in with our eyelids' as close as we could to the ground. The rockets would land and stones would fire like projectiles all over. Even though the rockets were aimed by the Taliban at the Americans, they would hit our base, the Italians, the Canadians and all the other nations that were out there as part of the bigger team.

During this time the British Army were training Afghan soldiers to fight and supporting them with their telecommunications. We would support with teleconferencing and introducing more sophisticated technology. Alongside this, we were working on a big operation, Camp Hero. It was a short distance from the Kandahar base. We would drive there, past half-built schools that had been halted as the war started. At this time, the British Army didn't have to carry weapons 'outside the wire' of Kandahar Airfield base. Other nations did, many who accompanied us. My role was working with a team at Camp Hero and setting up conferences, streaming, broadcasting and communication needs. We had a large stage and expensive kit and had to ensure the kit stayed there as things did go missing and there could be mistrust. Dutch soldiers accompanied us at the time, who carried weapons. I remember we slept on the stage the night before a big conference and my Dutch comrade gave me his weapon to sleep with. The event went well and we celebrated with amazing goat curry and, what became known as 'foot bread', likely due to the traditional way it was kneaded in Afghanistan. It was these moments that helped make the constant threat of death and attack easier to manage.

There were a lot of attacks on the camps. As well as the rocket attacks, there were suicide runs where people would infiltrate the base and climb into vehicles or also attempting to crash into military planes that were landing at Kandahar airport. Eventually, we had to carry weapons too. There was a police base outside of the camp that we often went to, again supporting with comms. The Afghan Army and police were very different and from separate regions. There always seemed to be friction between the two.

Whilst in Afghanistan, the forces would pay the locals for information including knowledge of any bombs and explosives in the area. One time, a local brought a large container which must have been a fertiliser bomb. He had brought it to the front gate of the camp. If it had exploded, it would have wiped out a large amount of the camp, including us, who were sleeping outside at the time. I remember towards the end of my first time in Afghanistan, having the overwhelming feeling that I was going to die. We had achieved so much in Afghanistan, building an operational centre for the whole of the command and supporting essential communications.

From this tour I received my general coins; a Dutch coin, an American coin and a NATO medal. I also received a thank you and acknowledgement letter from General Sir Nick Carter, former head of the UK's armed forces, with his coin, which spurred me on.

I returned to Germany from Afghanistan to my wife and children. I stayed in my posting at Herford for two years, during which time, I led a lot of adventure training. I completed and then taught a rock climbing course, which was great fun. During this time, I was also promoted to sergeant. After my Senior Commanders course, I was sent on tour to Afghanistan again in 2011/2012. This time, based in Camp Bastion, I was supposed to be dealing with one communications system. I desired a bigger challenge and I knew there was a digital surveillance system going out to be supported across Helmond at the time. I convinced my superiors to allow me to be part of the team going out there. I was always proactive and technically savvy and this must have been respected for them to change their minds.

Me, talking to Children in the poppy fields, Afghanistan
(2012)

I became part of the surveillance system's support team
and the detachments across Helmand Province. There would
be an operator in the Artillery that held technology and
cameras for intelligence gathering and deterrence. A large
mass would be erected with huge cameras that could see for
miles, along with smaller cameras for shorter field
surveillance. Balloons would be released with cameras
attached, aerostats. It was all interconnected. We were
attached to the Artillery Battery in Bastion 2 to provide the
technical expertise from the Royal Signals. Work
commenced maintaining the surveillance system. We were a
team of three sergeants and we all had roles alongside corporals and lance corporals. We would travel to where the
surveillance equipment was needing attention, at all hours of
the day. Going to these sites even meant patrolling on foot to
the area where the surveillance equipment was. One time we
were at a site near a poppy field and some children came
over. As a father myself, it was hard seeing the children.
They have nothing and played games with stones as their

toys. The children followed us and were laughing and playing, knowing no different. It was upsetting, acknowledging they were growing up around conflict, danger and having so little. Innocence clinging on around trauma, chaos and devastation.

Whilst I was in Camp Bastion, I instigated Operation Newcastle. The communication system that linked the surveillance sites wirelessly was a large broadcast of IP data, to put it simply, this decreased efficiency. There was an industry project due to come in to upgrade the system, which would have cost millions initially and in the long term. Ironically, I ended up working for a company after leaving the forces who would have been involved with this project and they never let me forget that we (I) took the work away! I devised a plan for all of the detachments across Helmand, using existing capabilities in an agile way, with zero downtime throughout the reconfiguration. The project worked and I increased the quality along with efficiency of the system. I was eventually awarded the Queen's Commendation for Valuable Service (QCVS) for this work.

Me, in Afghanistan (2009)

This was a great honour and I was pleased as part of a team we had improved the systems and safety of our military. There was the other side of the coin in that improved processes and systems of any kind, produced better outputs, in this case, kills. I remember a major saying that the number of kills associated with what we had done had massively increased. I know this would have saved lives on our side but it still felt like a punch in the stomach. We would see from the screens, people getting killed, day in and day out. The tragedy was that this included civilians, and children. The reality of war.

We weren't there to kill, it was a deterrent but it became 'kill TV.' People became disassociated and when I was told about the increase in kills, part of me died. We aren't trained to see people as someone's child, father, or mother. But that's what they are.

I was effectively congratulated on something that killed more people and I remember that being the catalyst for me to know I needed to get out.

The medals and coins I received in the army

I returned from Afghanistan and went back to adventure training. I began looking for jobs around the work I was doing. Luckily, I found a job outside of the army, with a supportive company who were prepared to wait for me to leave the army. At that time, the army was offering early release, I took the opportunity to forego any resettlement training as a result. There was a welfare officer in post and I remembered at the end of an adventure training session asking to speak to them and getting 'fobbed off'. I knew I needed some emotional well-being support but 'my ask' wasn't answered. It confirmed I was doing the right thing, leaving the army. I went into the offices in the summer of 2012, logged into the admin system and signed myself off from the army. Just like that. A click in a box as if online shopping. No one asked me what my motives really were as to why I was leaving, I wish they had. I know I was just a number, but it had still been a large part of my life.

Brothers in arms – Me, right.

My younger brother ended up joining the army, after I joined, and remains there this day. I am exceptionally proud of him, he has done very well in his army career and is a foreman of signals.

When I eventually left the army in September 2012, on my return to civvy street, I began working as a technical trainer and a system engineer. The readjustment was hard. I had known very little of adult life outside of the army. Places had changed in my hometown, people had changed. Friends had gone and some family members had passed away. Nothing was like it was those 11 years earlier, including myself.

I had to find who I was as a civilian, back in the town I knew so well but felt like a ghost in. My mental health wasn't good and I struggled to manage it. My marriage had broken down and I was angry with life. Asking for help isn't easy and I would hope over the years, it has become easier for veterans and anyone needing help. It was hard and I tried to deal with what played over in my head, what haunted and startled me.

Then I began a relationship with my now wife, Eve, a childhood school friend. She really helped me to find routine and purpose, but I still struggled mentally. I remember being out on one occasion at a local shopping centre with Eve and a vehicle went over a grate in the road, making a noise. I dived to the ground. Some things wouldn't stop replaying and I knew I had to seek help. I eventually went to see the doctor and I was diagnosed with Post-traumatic stress disorder (PTSD). I received some Talking Therapy which helped and I began to conquer the demons rather than the demons dominating me. It is not easy and there will always be triggers, but I manage it and I know there is support if I need it in the future.

Now I'm a lead engineer and love my role. My wife is a magnificent woman and we have a wonderful child together. I still see my children in Germany whenever possible. We've recently moved house and the future feels full of potential and happiness. I visit Operation Veteran, an organisation that has really supported me, when I can and it is great to see the other veterans and know there is a place for support. I am also part of a local veteran's cycle club which is a brilliant way to keep connected and healthy.

My memories of my time in the army remain close to my heart. I experienced some things I would hope no one ever does but at the same time, things that will stay with me for the right reasons. My children, friendships made, travel, resilience, loyalty, opportunity and a sense of pride. The army helped shape me as a person and I will forever be grateful for that.

Dedicated to all service persons past, present and future and their families. May their voices live on in these stories.

Love at First Sight
Norman Matthew Young

Name: Norman Matthew Young
Age: 83 years old
Armed Forces, Regiment / Rank: RAF, entered as Private / Gunner Driver left as SAC Senior Aircraftman
Date entered: June 1960
Date left: June 1962

I was one of the last batches of people to complete national service, serving my requirements in the Royal Air Force (RAF). Due to being a mechanic, a much needed skill at the time, I was deferred or I would have served my two years compulsory national service four years earlier. So by the time I did my national service, I was almost 21 years old. The authorities asked me what I would like to do in the armed forces and naturally I wanted to work with vehicles, so I said, "Drive." I was chosen as a gunner driver in the RAF.

My receiving camp base was Warrington, where I was chosen for the Queen's Colour Squadron, a unit which conducts ceremonial guard of honor duties. I was posted to

Catterick to complete my 12 weeks training, then I was on the move again onto Uxbridge, where I spent the rest of my service.

I entered the RAF as a single, young man. I came out of the RAF after two years, as a married man. I say single, I was technically engaged to a young lady named Joan, at home in Newcastle. However, that all changed the moment my eyes saw the magnificent beauty of my wife to be, my destiny and soul mate, my Gaynor.

Me, Uxbridge (1961)

It was Christmas Eve. I was on guard duty and this tiny, beautiful woman arrived. She was five foot nothing and weighed down with bags, almost toppling her short frame over! She had a hold-all, a bag on her shoulder and another bag clasped in her hand. Overloaded but still going. A strength she had her whole life, immediately evident.

I rushed over, offering to assist her to her billet. She advised me she was going to be posted at Uxbridge, as part of the RAF Police. I carried her bags, chatting as we walked and I wished the walk to her billet was miles away so I could talk to her for longer. Reluctantly leaving her at her billet, I smiled, reiterating I was on duty and if she needed anything, to let me know. She smiled back, the most magnetic, stunning smile with her mouth and kind eyes, illuminous like stars in the dark night sky. A smile I was lucky enough to witness thousands of times during all those years together.

I walked back to my station, grinning like a schoolboy at a

silly joke. It was love at first sight, I remember it vividly, even though it was over 60 years ago.

That weekend, I early returned to Newcastle, able to get a weekend off as I was still training. I ended the engagement with Joan, telling her I had met the woman I was going to marry. I sounded crazy, Gaynor and I had barely spoken. She had captured my heart and I knew she would be the only woman I could ever marry. If I couldn't have her, no other woman would do.

Gaynor, Uxbridge (1961)

Gaynor proved to be a challenge! It took me three weeks of asking, pestering and begging her to go on a date with me. She eventually agreed to go out with me, on her birthday, 27th January 1961. The perseverance paid off and Gaynor and I became not only a couple, but the best of friends.

We would visit the West End in London, seeing theatre productions. Some of which Gaynor even starred in as an actress, which was a part time job she acquired. We would visit the Palladium, the Hippodrome and more. We would watch the latest show, followed by a delicious meal in one of London's many restaurants. Life was good.

My own post in the RAF meant that when guard duties were not needed, I had a lot of free time. We had a number of guard duties and I met the Queen on a few occasions. One time in Heathrow, we were on duty and the Queen began walking along the line of guards, she came to me and asked how I was enjoying my role. We had polite chat and it was wonderful to speak to Her Majesty. We would train everyday, then if no guard of honor duties were scheduled, I was able to pick up part time work elsewhere to supplement the £1.50 per week wages I received from the RAF. I worked at a local firm, Norman Reeves, a Ford car garage. I loved cars and working with them felt as natural as breathing.

The free time Gaynor and I had allowed us to enjoy the area and nearby London. Many memories were made, times I treasure and times that somedays feel like yesterday and somedays feel like a lifetime ago. We had an amazing life together.

In Autumn 1961, Gaynor got notice that she was going to be posted to Cyprus. She nervously told me, clutching her hands together, her eyes willing for me to find an answer. We couldn't be separated, not now. She had become my whole life, and I hers. Our love could stand anything but the thought of being apart felt almost too much to bear. So perhaps quicker than we would have initially planned for our relationship, we got pregnant, meaning Gaynor wouldn't be posted to Cyprus. We got married on March 3rd 1962, in Uxbridge Registry Office. One of the happiest days of my life. Gaynor looked breathtaking and I was the proudest man in the world to have this wonderful woman as my wife.

We began married life in Hillendon, renting a home from a local German lady, who became a friend. Our first son, Matthew, was born June 1962 and not long afterwards, we decided to return to my home town of Newcastle. Moving to a flat in Jesmond, we settled and I got a job in Kenton Garage.

Our second son, Kevin was born in 1963 and we moved again to Killingworth, North Tyneside. I began working at Sunblest as a driver and stayed there for around seven years. Our youngest son Paul, was born during this time, in 1965. Life was good and our home always felt that love was part of the furniture.

In Autumn 1969, we were blessed with a baby girl, Ann-Marie. Our family felt complete. Sadly, tragedy struck and our daughter died suddenly on New Year's Day 1970. It was the most horrendous of times that resulted in many years of painful grief for us both, as well as our sons. Gaynor, understandably, was heartbroken. The night it happened played over and over in my mind many times for years. I can still picture it so vividly and for numerous years after her death, I had nightmares about my daughter.

It was New Year's Eve and we had a fresh year around the corner to look forward to. Ann-Marie had gone to sleep as normal then the next morning I went to check on her in her cot and she was extremely hot. She died there on New Year's Day, 1970 at 8:40am.

Gaynor and I on our wedding day (March 3, 1962)

There had been no symptoms or health concerns the night before or the days leading to Ann-Marie's death. We called the police and ambulance and after they arrived, they started their procedure of asking questions. We only had so many answers, it was unexplainable. Our own search for answers played on repeat in our heads. What had happened to our healthy baby girl?

Gaynor was distraught, hysterical. She ran from the house, in her bare feet and was later found miles away, inconsolable. She was taken to St. George's Psychiatric Hospital in Morpeth, where she remained for 19 months and her hair turned white overnight, due to shock and distress. Part of

Gaynor died when Ann-Marie passed, she never fully healed and the void for our daughter became the missing piece of her jigsaw that could never be replaced or found.

I left my job to look after our three young sons. Luckily, my sister lived next door to us and could support with child-care whilst I visited Gaynor in St. George's. It was a locked ward, with strict visitation controls and some very poorly people as patients. Each time I would visit Gaynor, a terribly distressed woman would run and try and grab me. She had been jilted at the alter and it had triggered a mental ill health episode. She would sob and sob, pain pouring out through her eyes. It was an awful place, with some extremely distressing stories and lost souls. In those days, there wasn't the help there is now. The professionals did what they could, but medicine has advanced, treatments are more sophisticated and society more understanding of people's mental wellbeing. It was a very challenging time for myself as a husband and father, and as someone grieving himself. But love can get people through anything and I loved my Gaynor with all my heart. I knew she would be ok, eventually.

Months passed and Gaynor continued getting treatment. In those days it was electroconvulsive therapy (ECT) where an electric current was sent through the brain of a patient, causing a brief surge of electrical activity, a seizure, in the brain. Although still used today in some settings, it was often used unethically in the 1970's, without anesthetic and without consent. Gaynor had 14 courses of this treatment and lived the rest of her life with scars on the side of her head where the invasive treatment had been administered.

When Gaynor eventually left hospital, she continued to struggle to manage her mental health. There was no community support, and the local GP could only do so much. Over the early years of losing Ann-Marie, Gaynor slashed her own wrists and took overdoses on a number of occasions, which would result in being hospitalized again. I felt helpless as I watched the woman I loved struggle like an injured puppy.

Gaynor's mother lived in Wales. I wondered if a fresh start, away from the reminders in our community of our trauma, could help Gaynor heal. I contacted her mother and asked if she could help secure us a council house in Wales. She did and we were offered a house in a town called Plas Madoc, a place between Wrexham and Llangollen.

I packed up our life, alone. Taking all of our belongings, our memories and the boys in a van, I collected Gaynor from the psychiatric hospital, and we left. For a new life, what I hoped would be a fresh start and a healing for my tortured wife, in Wales. The boys went to school near Wrexham, an ex-grammar school, Ysgol Ruabon. We settled and things got better, on the whole.

Gaynor was up and down, she struggled at times. Sometimes it was anniversaries, sometimes for no other reason that the fact grief had become an unwelcomed house guest. She would be medicated, tablet after tablet, prescription after prescription – diazepam, anti-depressants. They dulled the pain, but it never went away. Her struggle never stopped and she would lash out at the people she loved most. Although I knew she meant no harm, Gaynor was sometimes so full of pain that it seeped out of her. One time she stabbed me in the back. I have a scar and found a blade in her handbag a few years after she passed. I tried to keep the house safe, Gaynor, the boys and myself safe. It was hard and there was little help. Her heart was broken. It never healed. Her parents were a great support and they loved me as part of their family. Despite our challenges, my heart was always full of love for Gaynor. She was my world; my boys and her.

We returned to the North East in the 1980s. My mother

passed and the boys were grown up. I worked long hours to provide money for the boys to study, then once the boys went their own way, Gaynor and I decided to move again.

Derby was the next place to call home. We went for a new job opportunity for myself, followed by Gaynor also getting a job at the same place. We worked there together, happily for a number of years before Gaynor became poorly. I took early retirement as Gaynor's mobility deteriorated. We were offered a property on the Isle of Wight through SSAFA (Soldiers, Sailors, Airmen and Families Association). Here we lived for 22 years, the longest we had settled anywhere. In the last few years there, Gaynor's health worsened. She had numerous hospital stays, one lasting four months before our son, Matthew came to visit us on the Isle of Wight.

Myself and Gaynor; Gaynor's 65th birthday, 2008 at Newcastle United Football Club

Gaynor required further treatment for her health but there was little medical intervention that could help. She died of sepsis at home a few months later in 2018. When she was ill, I promised Gaynor that her final resting place would be with our daughter, Ann-Marie, in Benton, North Tyneside. We cremated my wife on The Isle of Wight, and I returned to the North East of England with her ashes to commemorate her and place her with her beloved daughter. I still visit her now, although she's always with me, in my head and heart. I keep busy, where I live, I have friends and the Operation Veteran groups mean I have company, laughs and I'm never too lonely. It's a different kind of busy, a distraction from grief, but I am grateful for it.

Me, on one of the many Operation Veteran beach walks
(2022)

We travelled a lot. In a way I think we were searching. Searching for something that put a plaster over our wound. But we never found it, no matter what we tried. Gaynor was my life. Married for 57 years, she was my one and only. We had it all; trust, love, laughter, even the sad times. A beautiful family, our boys grew up, went to university or into work. I have three grandchildren and my boys have grown up to be wonderful men, who I am extremely proud of. Once the boys were older, Gaynor and I travelled, despite her reluctance to fly. We drove around Europe in our Toyota Corolla, holidaying in Monte Carlo, Paris and Barcelona. I loved driving and Gaynor loved being a passenger, watching the scenery. Precious times.

And I have the memories, good and bad, mainly good. I carry them with me and I'm lucky to have found such love. My National Service became so much more, it became the beginning of my love story. I wish it could have lasted longer, 57 years doesn't feel long enough and I think of my Gaynor every day.

Dedicated to Gaynor Young.

To Chase a Dream

Peter Anthony Craigen

Name: Peter Anthony Craigen
Age: 76 years old
Armed Forces, Regiment / Rank: British Army, Royal Northumberland Fusiliers, Lance Corporal. Territorial Army, Home Service Force.
Conflicts / Tours served: Aden, Northern Ireland
Date entered: Feb 1965
Date left: Regular Army; Feb 1974. Territorial Army; 1982.

I was born in Walker, Newcastle and we lived above Smith's sweet shop, next door to the Army Drill Hall. I could see the band field from my house and I was mesmerised and inspired watching the military drills, dreaming of the day I could participate. As soon as I was old enough, I joined the cadets, full of energy and eagerness to learn. I remained in the cadets for a few years, before I started an apprenticeship as a moulder when I was 15 years old. It was a dirty job and I didn't enjoy it, I still had the seed of being in the military, growing in my mind.

I joined the Territorial Army and became part of the Drums. It was amazing and gave me a deeper insight into how life could be in the regular army. I was determined and in 1964, I went to the recruiting office in Newcastle and signed up. Some friends accompanied me, signing up also. One of those was Andy Parker, a childhood pal who I had many a good night out with frequenting Newcastle's Guys and Dolls Club and visiting the City Hall to see regular music shows staring Bobby Vee, Little Eva, Cilla Black and more.

We went back early the next year, 1965, to swear our Oath of Allegiance. I was 19 years old and we were given a coin and a Bible with the date inside, which I still have. I was raring to go and got off the starting blocks when basic training commenced, for around three months at the fusiliers training depot in Birmingham. There were several branches in training, Northumberland Fusiliers, Warwick Fusiliers, Lancashire Fusiliers and City of London Fusiliers. The different areas could be distinguished by the colour on their hackle, attached to our headwear, ours being red and white. Regardless of the regiment, we were proud of our hackle, but we wouldn't get to wear it until we had completed our basic training.

Basic training was difficult. Everything was timed, strictly and with discipline. Sometimes you got just two, short minutes to get into uniform or five minutes to shower and get ready. The race against time made the heart also race! It was a challenge, but I enjoyed the training. On completion and after receiving the red and white hackle I was so desperate to get, I was given my first posting. In May 1965 I was sent to Lemgo, Germany to join the battalion based there. On my first day, I remember getting a strict telling-off for not coming to attention. A lesson quickly learnt. In those first days, I saw prisoners of war blown across the street with water cannons.

Being naive at the time, I wondered what I had gotten myself into as I watched, mouth agape. Prisoners were also made to run up and down hills, just outside of Lemgo, carrying massive logs. The local press nicknamed us the Gestapo Fusiliers.

One time I was walking around Lemgo Square and I remember hearing the Laurel and Hardy theme tune. It was the army band playing. I was in the Corps of Drums myself, but not playing this tune at the time. It was a comical moment I still remember. The Drums were as regimented as many others and I remember tedious tasks like polishing my boots until I could literally see my face in them, reflecting like the sun on a puddle. Everything had to be spic and span, there was no room for error and if there was error or imperfection, you soon knew about it.

Me, top left - Army training depot, Birmingham (1965)

At the end of 1965, the battalion left Germany and

returned to Kirton in Lindsey, Lincolnshire. Here we stayed for around six months before being posted to Aden, Yemen, flying across in VC10's. It was 1966, The World Cup year! Luckily I got to see it before we were deployed.

On our arrival in Aden, it felt excruciatingly hot. I thought it was the engine of the VC10, situated at the back of the plane, near to where I was sitting. I was wrong, it wasn't the plane but the climate of Aden. I'd never known heat like it. We arrived at our base in Aden, Waterloo Barracks or Waterloo Lines as it was referred to, taking over from another battalion and this happened throughout the postings.

Patrols began, as we accustomed ourselves to the area and the climate, as much as we could coming from cold, wet England. Our main area was Crater, a city in the bowl of an extinct volcano, surrounded by high cliffs. At Kirton in Lindsey, we had chalked out the streets of Crater, on the floors of the old RAF hangers, helping us get an idea of where we may be sent to. Our own map.

The main weapon from the enemy was grenades. Shrapnel from the grenades was boiling hot and caused damage and there were many injuries as a result. Rifles were also carried by the terrorists. During the posting, the six-day war occurred, between Egypt and Israel. At this time, we got confined to the barracks on occasion. There was an undercurrent, something that was happening without us knowing.

Then on 20th June 1967, the Arabian Army mutiny happened. Many of our comrades had left Aden, returning home. Some were at Khormaksar airport waiting to leave. We had stayed on a little longer but were also almost ready to depart, having served our time, with the new regiment arriving to replace us. One of the main roads in Crater City, Queen Arwa Road had the armed police barracks situated on it at the time. On the morning of the 20th the Argyll Sutherland Highlanders were in camp, taking over from us. We were showing them our patrol, one of our last tasks before we would leave.

On this morning, Arab soldiers of the South Arabian Army mutinied. One of our patrols went in and was ambushed. Then another patrol went in to help and was also attacked. The soldiers did their duty in very dangerous circumstances and sadly, all members of the two patrols were killed.

All our comrades at the airport, waiting to come home, returned. We got ready for battle. Our group was coming back to Crater from Fort Morbut. I remember, when we were driving to Crater, we saw an armoured personnel carrier, pig as we referred to them, with one of its wheels shot out in an attack. We approached the armoured vehicle where there was a soldier in the back who looked in an exhausted daze, his face covered in dark, oily sweat. The vehicle had been attacked and it could have been us in the firing line, had we continued on our journey. It was a disturbing day that still haunts me.

That day in Crater, 12 soldiers in two patrols were killed by the South Arabian Armed Police. A further 13 people were killed later in connection to this, including a civilian. All the soldiers were from the Northumberland Fusiliers, the Royal Core Transport or the Argyll Sutherland Highlanders with 9 of our regiment killed.

After returning to the Kirton in Lindsey, Lindsey I began training with the Mortars and in 1967 on New Year's Eve, I met my wife-to-be Anne. She was from Wallsend and worked at Thermal Syndicate, a factory producing heat-resistant materials. We clicked, a natural connection and began spending time together.

However, in January 1968, I was posted to Northern Ireland. At the time my mother took ill and I was really worried. They called us the 'Fusilier family' and they were exactly that. I remember us all being asked separately about our well-being by our mortar officer. I mentioned I was concerned about my mother's health and within a few months of being in Northern Ireland, I was given a posting in Fenham Barracks, back in Newcastle. This allowed me to care for my mother, live at home and commute to work. It also gave Anne and I the opportunity of time together and we became inseparable. She was my sunshine on even the coldest of North East England days.

Whilst I was posted to Fenham Barracks, we used to go on tour across the North East, showcasing the army and encouraging people to sign up. I did this for a few years but by 1974, I had decided to come out of the forces. On hearing I was leaving, 101 Regiment, Royal Artillery advised me I would become a full sergeant in six months if I remained in the army. By this time Anne and I were serious. We had three daughters (Anne's from a previous relationship, that I very much saw as my children). After the horror I had seen in Aden and knowing of the destruction that happened after I left Northern Ireland, I wasn't keen to stay in the army and perhaps be posted to a place of conflict. I had witnessed the death of comrades, knowing they had wives and children they were leaving behind. I had sympathy for partners and wives worried about their loved one out at war and didn't want that for Anne. Love and responsibility made me see the world through different eyes.

Me, top row, third from left. Corps of Drums, St George's Day (1968).

I left the army and joined Anne, working at Thermal Syndicate. Alongside my job at Thermal Syndicate, I joined the TA in the Home Service Force which was established to defend home shores. I was part of the team for eight years, before it disbanded and I left the armed forces in 1982.

In 1977, Anne and I got married. We had a wonderful marriage and went on to have a son, meaning we had four loving children. I now have a total of 18 grandchildren and great-grandchildren. I have to keep all their birthdays on a calendar, or else I would forget!

After a while at Thermal Syndicate, I decided I wanted to go into social care. I studied in Newcastle and ended up getting a job as a residential care officer for a company in North Tyneside, working in a children's home in Whitley Bay. It was a home for girls with behavioural and emotional difficulties, many of whom had experienced early childhood trauma. We provided support within the accommodation and also supported young people in the community, in their own tenancies. The young people were vulnerable, it was our job to try and build their resilience and keep them safe. It was a rewarding job but not without challenges. The highs and lows swung like a pendulum. It could be frustrating due to the lack of resources available for young people but it was also exhausting emotionally at times. I worked within children's services for around 15 years, before taking voluntary redundancy.

After this, I worked in concierge for a few years but it wasn't for me, so I took early retirement. I volunteered with the North East Ambulance Service as a driver, supporting people to access appointments at hospital. I remember one time, a guy I had been taking for treatment told me he had to organise his Christmas cards. I was taking him home from an appointment where he had just be told he only had a few weeks to live. These instances made me value life. I hope in some way, the small talk and smiles I offered helped people in their time of need. Eventually, I stopped volunteering and retired completely.

Anne was offered retirement not long after. We were in our early 60s and we were living in a caravan park in Northumberland. With good pensions and time on our hands, we began travelling the world. New Zealand, Australia, Hong Kong, Canada, and Europe, we visited so many places. Malta was our favourite and I have precious memories from such good times, filled with smiles and love. We had a memorable time in Hong Kong at the races where we place a £1 bet on four horses and won about £2,500 converted into UK pounds!

Another lucky occasion, we were in Canada, staying in Banff in The Rockies and were due to move on to our next destination. However, there had been a storm and the roads

Anne and me in Malta (2014)

were flooded so we had to remain where we were for a further night. It eased a little that evening, so Anne and I went out we found the local Canadian Legion club. It was bingo night so we joined in, sitting next to a local woman who helped us get started. We ended up winning house, over $1000. I gave the lady at our table a little money for helping us and bought the bar staff a round of drinks. Another of the many great memories that I cherish.

Anne and I had been together about 50 years when it was discovered she needed a quadruple heart bypass. We had gone to the hospital for a pre-op meeting and they advised us she had to stay in. Anne was in the hospital for around four days, being moved from a single room to a ward. In the ward someone was quite poorly, coughing lots. It made me feel uneasy and the next day she was transferred to another hospital for the procedure. The operation was scheduled and cancelled. The re-scheduled operation was cancelled as Anne had developed a cough. It was cancelled again and then on the fourth occasion, the operation went ahead. However, after three days post-surgery, Anne began going downhill, sepsis was mentioned but not documented. Something wasn't right, I could tell. I knew my Anne. I was told she was fine by hospital staff, even after I expressed concern.

The next morning I received a phone call from the hospital advising me to come in as Anne was very unwell. I rushed to the hospital and Anne was taken to ICU. I was told by one of the doctors that we would know in a few days as to whether Anne would make it or not. She was on oxygen and hooked up to various machines. I recall it was a Wednesday of that week when I received a phone call from the hospital. I knew what was happening so rang the family. About a dozen members of the family managed to come to the hospital and we decided to turn the machines off. Anne and I had previously talked about her wishes and she had made it clear that if her health deteriorated, she would want life support turned off. I followed her wishes. It was the hardest thing I have ever done in my life and five years later, it still hurts to remember. At 14:45, on that awful day in March 2017, Anne was gone, aged 75. Part of me died with her.

I felt like the hospital had been negligent and I tried to pursue it for three years, to no avail and in the process, being let down by incompetent legal support. I could have tried again but we wanted to grieve as a family. It had been an awful few years and I still miss Anne every day. I hold onto my memories. I visit her at the cemetery 4-5 times a week and a void has been left in my world that will never be filled. I am grateful I have my

Me, middle, with the Association on St George's Day (2012)

family and also the Fusilier Association as well as Operation Veteran and the people where I live. Within the Association, there are people I served with in 1965 who I met again 40 years later. We have been on battlefield trips all over the world as a group and have had some wonderful times together. We keep in touch and meet monthly as well as the trips.

I joined a veterans allotment in Wallsend, where I saw my old pal, Andy Parker. It was like it had only been yesterday and not all those decades ago. I also renewed a friendship with Terry Burn, who attends the allotment and Operation Veteran. The saying 'once a Fusilier, always a Fusilier,' was never more apt.

I keep busy, I'm lucky in that I have company, but nothing and no one can ever replace Anne.

Me and my friend Terry, Queen Elizabeth II memorial service (2022)

Dedicated to Anne Craigen.

Second Chances
Robert (Bob) Daniel McCarthy

Name: Robert (Bob) Daniel McCarthy
Age: 80 years old
Armed Forces, Regiment / Rank: Royal Air Force.
Senior Aircraftman - Catering
Conflicts / Tours served: Borneo
Date entered: June 1962
Date left: Dec 1971

I had eagerly been waiting for my National Service call-up papers to be delivered and they never arrived. Each morning I would check the post, to no avail. In the end, I visited the recruiting office, stamping my feet to discover there had been a temporary hold on call-up. They advised me that there was a backlog of people waiting to finish courses at college and they weren't recruiting for the armed forces at that time. I sighed, my mindset was joining the military, I didn't want to wait and continue with the mundane, unrewarding job I had.

The recruiting officer looked at me, seeing disappointment etched across my face and advised me I could join as a regular instead of through the National Service process.

"Where do I sign?" I immediately asked.

At the time, I had an awful job as a polisher. It was a tedious and filthy role, with no job satisfaction. I polished brass, day in day out. There were never masks and dust flew all over. I worked with a lot of older men who advised me to join the military and get out of polishing. Many had been in the forces and informed me that signing up for the armed forces was the best thing I could do to give me independence and a career. I recall when I was accepted into the RAF, the oldest man I worked with as a polisher, Harry, gave me a set of rosary beads. He told me they were his late wife's. It was a moving gesture of protection and I've always remembered his kindness.

I began my career at the RAF, completing training at Bridgnorth, Wolverhampton. After my training I was posted to Hereford, followed by Horsham St. Faiths in Norwich then back to Hereford, where I stayed until November 1962. I completed my catering training before being posted to RAF St Athens, in Wales. I loved Wales, it was a beautiful place and I have fond memories of it. At the time I had recently gotten married. My first wife was with me in Wales, even though we couldn't get living quarters as there were so many people there. After Wales, I was posted to Borneo, leaving my wife behind.

A vivid and dangerous memory sticks in my mind from that time. Looking back it sounds very comical but at that moment, it was more than one narrow escape! One of the lads, Rod, had a fascination with the Dalia Lama, Buddhism and spirituality. He would often spend time in deep meditation. He used to talk about his beliefs and how he would go into a trance, keeping him grounded. When we were in Borneo, he told us that they had built a new mosque and he wanted to visit it. That it was meant to be the most stunning building; white with a gold roof. We had been in Borneo for ten months and hadn't had any leave. The officer came to me one day and mentioned I hadn't taken any time off. I jokingly questioned where I could go, we were on an island after all! Then I

thought about Rod and his desire to visit the new mosque. I asked the officer if I could have a few days off to visit the mosque with Rod. The plan was made, Rod was delighted and I was intrigued by something different.

The next day Rod and I set off on our adventure, eager like school kids and pleased to have a bit of time away from the regimented routine of daily life in base camp. We got on a small paddle steamer boat and travelled to a place called Jesselton.

Me in the RAF (1962)

On arrival, we excitedly disembarked and then looked at each other, not knowing which way to go. A group passed us, a teacher with some 18-year-old female students. It was a sight for us indeed, after spending so much time with just males. Although I was married, Rod looked on at the girls, mouth open. The teacher was less than impressed as we went toward him, clearly thinking we were going to try and approach the girls. Waving a cane in our direction, he indicated for us to go away. We explained that we simply wanted directions to the mosque. He abruptly pointed us in the direction, watching us like a hawk as we set off, away from the students.

Rod and I went on our merry way, entertained by the

performance and a great start to our trip. As we moved in the
direction of the mosque, the jungle growth began to get
denser. It didn't put us off, we were fuelled by our time away
from camp and the adrenalin of our expedition. Continuing
through the thickening jungle, we chatted about life and our
hopes and dreams. It soon began to get dark, even though it
was only mid-afternoon. Pausing for a moment, we contemplated going back. Scratching my head as Rod put a hand on
his chin, it dawned on us; we didn't know which direction we
had come, or which direction to go.

Despite completing robust, rigorous training that made
the difference between life and death when in battle, we had
failed to bring any supplies. Deciding to continue, we kept
going until it was getting darker and darker, the night turning
velvety black. We decided to sleep under a tree, there were
certainly no beds nearby and we had to rest. Looking back, it
was so dangerous. The jungle was full of predators and we
were easy prey for humans and animals! With no provisions
and wearing civvy clothes, we felt very vulnerable as we tried
to cosy up together against the tree. During the night, we were
terrified by the constant noises. Animals growling, screeching
and creatures on the move. For all the bravery we had been
taught in the forces, we were flinching, holding our breath and
grabbing onto one another for most of the night.

The next morning after little to zero sleep, we felt like
zombies pulling ourselves up from the ground, groaning as our
back and legs screamed from the hard ground and our stomachs growled like the creatures we had listened to all night.
We began walking again with distinct evaporation of the
enthusiasm we had 24 hours earlier as we'd set off from camp.
Our energy was depleted and patience had flown off with the
birds from the trees. Then we saw it! The mosque. The beautiful white building with the gold roof stood proud like a soli-

taire diamond in a ring, there for people to gaze at in wonder. It gave us the energy we needed and we were smiling again. We walked up to the structure and around the building, trying to find a door to go inside, desperate to see the bounty of our hunt. There were several doors, but none would open. Someone eventually came out and told us we couldn't come in due to our attire. So that was the end of our mosque adventure. Seen from the outside only, like a magnificent cookery programme that you will never taste the food from.

Shaking our heads, off we set again, to try and find our way back to the shore to return to camp. The jungle was so copious, we were cutting vegetation back as we went with our parangs. Soon we came across a huge house on stilts about 40 feet long. Children were playing outside and came rushing up to us, eyes wide. Rod and I were exhausted, hungry and wished for home, our camp. All of a sudden, two of the children climbed up a tree, chopped a coconut off and climbed back down with ease as if they were walking up a flight of stairs. They must have only been about five years old and one reached for a knife. In the blink of an eye, he chopped open the coconut and passed it to us. The milk felt like liquid heaven as we closed our eyes and let it fill our mouths and stomachs.

The adults had arrived by this point and the maidens were walking around with no clothing on, except a small cloth covering their genitals. The camp leader spoke pigeon English and told us in no uncertain terms that if we touched the maidens, they would chop our heads off. The males proceeded to show us around the camp, repeatedly warning us to stay away from the females. The camp leader pointed to a display of skulls, lined up like ornaments on a fireplace. Nervously, Rod and I nodded as we swallowed what felt like concrete in our throats and panic threatened to engulf us. The skulls looked too small to be animals but it was certainly not the time to ask about the artefacts like it was a museum tour.

We didn't want to stay, given the threat of being decapitated by the camp leader, however, we were also wary of leaving and looking ungrateful to our terrifying host, as well as the possible consequences of not accepting the hospitality with a side order of death threat on offer. We needed rest and food after a night of jungle horror! Getting our sheets, offered to us by the camp leader, we were shown to a bed. It was surrounded by dried palm leaves that would make a spectacular cracking and crunching noise if we were to stand on them. Trapped in our bed, in fear of getting up and becoming the target of their chopping practice, we had another restless night, terrified it would be game over at any time.

Eventually it was morning and the camp leader allowed us to go safely on our way. The relief of surviving another night in the jungle felt like winning the lottery as we scurried off, not looking back. We came to a track that looked well used, a positive sign for us and some much-needed luck for our nervous system. I pointed out that a bush was moving and the terror returned, thinking it could be a predator waiting for us. It was wavering as we got closer so we crept up with our weapons and out jumped a man shouting, 'HALT!' It turned out it was a Northumberland Fusilier, rifle in hand. We were delighted to see him and he updated us that they had made a small camp nearby as there was a sniper in the area taking pot shots at them.

The Gurkhas had alerted the army that we were within the surrounding area, they had 'felt our feet' and knew our movements. We hadn't even noticed. The army colonel gave us a telling-off before offering us a beautiful meal of casserole, which was much needed. We were offered camp beds and quickly went to sleep. When we woke up, we were back on our island in our billet, with no recollection of how we got there. I asked Rod if he had any memories of getting home and like myself, he didn't. We both thought we must have been drugged, which wouldn't be normal practice from the armed forces but both of us were in civvy clothes and could have been anyone. It remains a mystery to this day but an adventure I will never forget!

After 12 months in Borneo, I returned to Hereford, where I remained for six years. I worked in catering but also the training academy for new catering staff. It was nice to teach and mentor the recruits and I enjoyed my time there. I left after this and had mixed feelings about departing from the military. My wife and I had a child at this point and she wanted me to return to civvy street. Of course, I wanted to be with my family but it was still hard leaving something I had known for so long.

On leaving, I ended up working as an engineer with Hoover after a five-week training course. I remained in the engineering industry all my working life, even working part-time after retirement age. When I eventually retired completely, I worked for the local authority as a Mace-Bearer for the mayor. The mayor was ex-RAF, so it felt perfect for me. I enjoyed this role, it was very fulfilling. I still do it now, going to Worcester each Christmas for the fair, carrying the mace for the mayor. It's an honour, just like my time in the RAF was.

Me at the Malaya and Borneo Veterans AGM, Stafford (2013)

Seven years ago my wife sadly died and it was such a monumental loss to me. I had my children and grandchildren luckily and social interaction including being part of the Malaya and Borneo Veterans Association and that's where I met Gwen.

Dedicated to my wife, Gwen.

Name: Gwen McCarthy
Age: 77 years old

I began attending the Malaya and Borneo Veteran Association meet-ups with friends from the North Tyneside branch. It was a great way to socialise and I enjoyed the companionship as well as the appreciation of the armed forces. Bob was part of the Worcester branch and although we had both been to several events, we had never met each other.

Five years ago, there was a meet-up in Blackpool and that's where I first saw Bob. He was so handsome and as I watched him, he smiled at someone. It was such a warm, genuine smile like the sun coming through the clouds on a dreary day. I was mesmerised. During the rest of the weekend, we kept bumping into each other, at breakfast or lunch or during coffee.

I was smitten. Sunday came around far too quickly and it was time to leave. As usual, it had been a wonderful weekend, an absolute tonic to the soul. Everyone was saying their goodbyes and talking about the next meet-up. Bob was there and we said goodbye. I felt sad to be leaving him, he had made such an imprint on me just from a few interactions.

There was a reunion planned, the AGM in October and I was desperately hoping that Bob would be there. I was counting down the days like a child to their birthday! After meeting him in Blackpool, I had mentioned Bob to my daughter Joanne, a few times over the summer, saying I hoped I would see him again. My daughter was delighted to see me excited about a possible love interest and suggested I wrote a little card out for Bob, in case he was there. So I did, not knowing if I would have the bravery to hand it to him if I saw him. I wanted to make the right impression and be sensitive so I wrote in the card asking if Bob would like to be friends.

It turned out that Bob couldn't get booked in the hotel for the AGM. His daughter Rachel, kept ringing to try and secure a room. Luckily, Rachel managed to get a cancellation for Bob last minute and on arrival, Bob was the first person I saw. Butterflies took off in my stomach and I felt like a teenager, even in my early 70s!

We had a few smiles and small talk over the event and I struggled to build up the courage to hand Bob my card. However, at the end of the AGM, the group came out of the church parade and as we did, my daughter text at that exact moment. It was as if she knew. Bob was standing opposite me and the message from Joanne said, "Give him the card."

It felt like a sign and I walked over to Bob. Hands trembling, I gave him the card saying in a quiet voice it was for him to read at home. I felt like I was on a stage, giving a speech to thousands of people. But it was my chance and perhaps my only chance. I got a shock when he took my hand and led me towards the bar in the hotel where we had a quick chat and we got a photograph together.

Transport was waiting to take people home, so we exchanged phone numbers and left. I put my hands to my mouth, not quite believing what had just happened and feeling proud of myself for having the courage to make a move. Less than 24 hours later, Bob rang me, informing me he was coming to visit. That was it, we fell in love, although I was definitely already falling, a long time before I gave Bob the card.

Our relationship developed and Bob would travel up from Worcester and I would travel down, which took seven hours on the coach. We were in love and knew we wanted to be together, forever. Bob moved up to North Tyneside and we got married. Bob was 76 and I was 73 years old and we have now been married four years. We have six children, eleven grandchildren and two great-grandchildren.

We have so much in common; socialising, upcycling furniture and coming to Operation Veteran, where I have made friends with wives of veterans.

I never thought at my age I would have found love but I did, I took a chance on love and we have found our happy ever after.

Bob and myself, Buckingham Palace Garden Party, 2022

Time Passes, Camaraderie Remains

Terence (Terry) Burn

Name: Terence (Terry) Burn

Age: 67 years old

Armed Forces, Regiment / Rank: British Army – Boy soldier 15-17 years old, First Battalion Fusiliers, Corporal until 1979. Territorial Army (TA) Fusiliers, Sergeant Major until 1998.

Conflicts / Tours served: Gibraltar 1972 – 1973, Northern Ireland 1973 – 1975, Bermuda 1977, Cyprus 1978

Date entered: 1970

Date left: 1998

I joined the army at the age of 15, to prove my uncle wrong! I was born and bred in North Shields and my father worked at the shipyards. As a young boy, I had wanted to join the navy with my best friend, but my uncle had been to Aden, Yemen and said I wouldn't be able to handle the army. So being a 15-year-old, with a strong mind, I joined and in the process proved him to be mistaken.

Being so young, I started as a boy soldier and army life

was all I knew for many years. I enjoyed everything about the army and all it gave me as an individual. I knew when I left, I couldn't let it go completely. That's what led me to the TA and I was able to enjoy the best of both worlds; the military and civvy street.

After joining the army at 15 years old, I did two years of training at Shorncliffe, near Folkstone. After that, I had my first posting in Gibraltar, training with the regular unit from 1972-73. It was a new world, away from all I had known in North Tyneside and I felt lucky to be given the chance and filled with energy to be my best. In 1973, I was posted to Northern Ireland, where I remained for 18 months. It was during this time that I met my first wife, my beloved Ann.

When I went to Northern Ireland, I was still only very young, at 18 years old. Like most 18-year-old boys, I felt invincible, with an extra superpower of being a soldier! On my first tour, an incident occurred almost straight away. I had been there a matter of days and headed into a troubled area. I was greeted with a brick to the face and spent the subsequent few days in bed, stuck within the camp with stitches on my face. After this episode, luckily, I had no more trouble.

However, my parents had seen the atrocities and unrest in Northern Ireland and my dad tried to 'buy me out.' My parents had very little money, so this intention showed me how frightened they were for their son, their child. It must have been hard for them, I understand that now. Their son went into conflict, but the army was my life. It was the air in my lungs, the blood in my veins. People at home, across the world, only ever saw the bad news on TV. Of course, this is what sells newspapers and makes people watch the TV, but it's a snapshot of reality, a small piece in a much larger jigsaw. Comrades sitting around sharing stories of home, laughing, congratulating each other on a day of strength, teamwork and determination. This was much of the reality. Alongside this, the locals were great and weren't the enemy. That doesn't sell newspapers and doesn't make people want to tune into the news. For all the bad, the sad, and the sometimes mad, there were lots of positives and happy times. I understood they were frightened, as the snippets they saw on the news and in the press were filled with fear. Disturbing news, anxiety provoking and heartbreaking. But there was no way I was prepared to leave the army, well not alive anyway!

During my time in Northern Ireland, my wife-to-be, Ann, came over. She had also heard and seen the unrest and was understandably nervous. I completed three tours of Northern Ireland in total with my second, returning to Belfast. This posting was for four months in 1976 and was reasonably quiet. Then I returned to Northern Ireland for the third time in 1977, posted to guard the polling stations. On our arrival, we were shipped down to South Armagh as Captain Nairac, a British Army Officer had gone missing. We never discovered any evidence. It was believed he was abducted and killed by the Irish Republican Army (IRA). His body was never found.

I travelled the world with the army; Kenya, Bermuda and Cyprus. Stunning places, despite the tension, disturbances and unrest. In Bermuda there had been a period of riots, we were there for three weeks and then we went firefighting in London. During this time, there was a fireman's strike so the army was asked to help out. We completed one day of training at Catterick for firefighting, before being deployed to support.

My wife, who remained at home whilst I was posted to Bermuda, had written a letter to my parents saying we could not visit at Christmas. Being in Bermuda, it was unclear how long I could be posted. This was in 1977 and I still have her letter, a cherished note, as my wife passed away when she was just 40 years old, in 1995.

During my time in the forces, I was also posted to Cambridge. This was where I completed training at the school of engineering to be an Assault Pioneer. It assisted me to progress in the army and then also in the TA, where I took on the role of running assault pioneer Platoon for around 12 years. I got involved with parades including St George's Day and others with the Battalion. So many great memories with my comrades.

I came out of the army in 1978, after my last tour in Cyprus. I was 23 years old. It wasn't an easy decision, military life felt so natural to me, it was my whole working experience, even though I was still so young. The army was something I was good at and enjoyed. I was respected and respected my comrades. I had a purpose, identity and focus. However, I was also a husband and father and my family needed me. My wife and young son had remained in Newcastle, whilst I was on tour. It felt like the army was a single man's game and playing it as a husband and father didn't feel right to me, even if the military felt like my family also. I was offered pre-release training. The army had wanted me to stay and I received a letter after six to nine months of leaving, asking me to return.

By this point, I had already joined the TA. Army life was part of my DNA and I couldn't imagine my life without the forces. The TA allowed me to have that essential lifeblood of military work but also meant I was at home, with my family and I could join civvy street employment and spent most of my career driving.

Me, right, in the TA (Mid 1980s)

The TA was ideal for me, I enjoyed my roles immensely. I remember meeting a young lad who couldn't read or write. He wanted to learn engineering skills and I was determined to help him to succeed. It took patience, understanding and support. The lad ended up achieving his goals and passed his exams. When I first joined the TA, I was in charge of recruits and I recall having two recruits who couldn't read or write. If you couldn't read or write in the regular army, you wouldn't get in. I went to the major who commented that just because the two recruits couldn't read or write, it didn't mean they would not make good soldiers. He was absolutely right and the lads thrived in the TA. It was amazing to see some of the lads go through training and succeed, I loved being part of their training.

I was on the shooting team in the army. I never won anything but enjoyed being part of the team. In the TA I wanted to be the champion shot in the Battalion and win the cup, so I tried and tried, determined to win. At last, after what seemed an eternity, I won. However, no cup came my way. The cup I had dreamed of holding. Instead, they had changed the prize, from a cup to a weapon mounted on a plaque. The initial disappointment flew away with the wind when I realized I was the first in my Battalion to get this prize, so in fact, it was something quite special after all.

Life continued, the TA, Ann and my children. Ann had battled cancer and all seemed to be going well. However, she became poorly again. I had travelled to Germany with the TA and received notice after a few days to advise me she was very unwell. I returned home and we lost Ann a week later. The cancer she had so bravely conquered before, had returned and invaded her body, snatching her away from us. She was a wonderful woman and mother and I still miss her daily.

Ann and me, St George's Ball, TA

I was lucky enough to marry again and had another loving marriage with my second wife, Marie. Sadly, Marie also passed away. I am grateful for my time with both my wives and the beautiful family I have. Ann and I had two sons, both have done exceptionally well. One son went into the army and the other joined the police. I also have a wonderful stepdaughter and nine Grandchildren.

Many great times were had in the TA but eventually, it was time to leave. I left in 1998, aged 43 years old. I know many people who have been in the forces for numerous years and struggle to adjust and find their place in civvy street. Veterans feel lost in a society they can't click in to, bouncing around looking for purpose. Some don't have families or have ex-partners and children in other countries. Loneliness, a loss of identity, the camaraderie, you grieve for it all when you leave the forces.

It's hard. The TA really helped me with this transition and I would recommend it to anyone. The added bonus is that I would meet up with my old regiment in Germany, when travelling with the TA. I have friends I've served with who live all over the world. Some moved to different countries after meeting their wives on their tours. In 1991, whilst in the TA, I travelled to Gibraltar and I met some of the soldiers I had toured with in the regular army.

Me, left in Gibraltar (1991)

Now, I'm a member of the Association and we have travelled all over. We went to Cyprus and I met my old major from the army, after 30 years! The Associations and Operation Veteran are important to me. The military is a way of life, it's been such a massive amount of my time on earth and it will always be a part of my life. The Association meets monthly and we have a veteran's allotment in Wallsend. It was set up last year and it is a massive part of my week. It is great to see the vegetables and fruit grow, meet up with the veterans and get fresh air and exercise. It nourishes me in more ways than the food produced.

Me left, with my friend Peter, at V.E Day Remembrance Ball, Blyth (2021)

I go for the weekly walks with Operation Veteran and come to the Thursday group. I've made friends and it is wonderful to talk about shared experiences. Our personal histories are all different but we share the understanding of the forces, the good and the bad. There is no other connection like it.

You leave the army and you have no rank, you are all the same. Time passes but friendship remains. Camaraderie stays strong and respect never dissolves.

Dedicated to Ann Burn.

The Value of Respect
Victor (Vic) Kenneth Thompson

Name: Victor (Vic) Kenneth Thompson
Age: 64 years old
Armed Forces, Regiment / Rank: Royal Marine Commando's, Sergeant.
Conflicts / Tours served: Tours of America, South Pacific, West Indies, Gibraltar, Norway
Date entered: April 1975
Date left: 1996

Military life was in my family, part of the DNA. My father, step-father and men before them all joined the Merchant Navy and from the age of eight years old, it was my dream to go to sea. When I was around 11 years old, myself and a friend started going down to the Fish Quay dock in North Shields, asking the fishermen if we could go on the boats. We pushed our luck, pestering the workers in the hope that someone would feel sorry for two kids, desperate to go to sea. A few times it paid off and it was like Christmas Day being on those boats. I found my first love, the sea!

I eventually joined the forces in 1975. Myself and a school friend had both been in the Sea Cadets and I was ready for full-time work and to travel. The cadets was an adventure, it made me feel alive and I wanted more. We visited the Armed forces careers office in Newcastle to enquire about joining the Royal Navy. I had decided I wanted to be a cook at sea and told the recruiting officer this, who then brought another officer in to chat with me. I told them my whole dream had been to go to sea and this recruiting officer said to me, "If you are a Royal Marine Commando, you'll be at sea and get the best of both worlds."

I still had my exams to do at school but I was advised I could study for my exams alongside learning my commando training in the Royal Marines. The wonderful thing about the forces is that the education system is strong. The ability for someone to learn a specific trade such as catering, engineering or mechanics but also study other topics and essential qualifications. This and of course the life lessons the forces teaches you, you could search the world for and never find in a textbook. It's not easy, learning a trade, studying and being away from home. On top of that, you are becoming someone and something the forces want. If you can do it, I think you can do anything in life and you'll get an education like no other, both academically and in the school of life!

Joining the Royal Marines in 1975, I was sent to the Royal Marines depot in Deal to embark on the first part of my commando training. The Deal depot closed as a training base in 1977, with all training since being at Lympstone. Phase two was at Lympstone, which was operating alongside Deal, in 1974. The training for both phase one and phase two was nine months in total, a very intensive time, but a period of time that helped shape me for the next two decades in the

Royal Marines. After the training, I completed the course and graduated, or 'passed out' as it's known in the forces.

Royal Marines Motto dating back to 1775: Per Mare Per Terram (By Sea By Land) Me: Back row, in the middle in January 1976

During my training, I studied at the same time. It was a challenge and some days I felt like my brain alone was carrying a 100lb rucksack. But I found it easier than some. I would work through the day, participating in commando training then on an evening, each night, I would study. It was a good job there was little else to do and very limited distractions. We shared six-men rooms at the time but I could access the quiet room to study, absorbing the information, building my knowledge like the layers of a cake. It all eventually paid off and I passed all my exams. Discipline was all around, from the moment you woke up to the moment you went to sleep. Your daily routine, your commitment to developing, growing and to excel.

At the time there was a category of special entry level for

the Royal Marines. Due to this, the process was you would join and be allocated a job role they were short of. Therefore, you would complete basic training and do some commando training but not complete it. You would then progress into your specialist training, in my case to be a chef. This usually meant you couldn't graduate, or pass out with the Royal Marine Commando training as you didn't fully complete it. However, myself and another lad wanted to pass out and complete our training. It was going against the process but it was important we requested our desire. Luckily, it was granted, meaning I could pass out as a Royal Marine Commando before moving on to my catering training.

The Royal Marines basic training is the longest in duration of any infantry programme within NATO, 32 weeks in total. To achieve the end goal of wearing a green beret, all recruits must complete the 32 weeks training including a series of gruelling commando tests that include a 9 mile speed march, The Endurance Course, The Tarzan Assault Course and finally a 30 mile march across open ground in Dartmoor. The last test is completed in full fighting attire including bergen, within eight hours.

As a youngster, the Royal Marines opened my eyes. Despite it always being my childhood wish, that I would spend many an hour visualising, it was still a shock to the system. The training, the expectations, the critical nature of being regimented and following orders. It was hard, at times almost suffocating, but the achievement was exhilarating and many times I felt as if I had scored the winning world cup goal! Emotions and feelings like no others; both highs and lows.

Even before being drafted to my first posting, the training made me aware of what I could be going into, at any location in the world. My role, my purpose, my mission. For my first posting, I was stationed in Plymouth, commando logistics regiment then, 42 Commando. Joining a new unit, I went before the commanding officer, with sweaty palms and almost holding my breath. The commanding officer knew a great deal about his new recruits, from the file full of information about each new officer. This initial meeting filled me with dread, those critical first impressions counting. As my time in the Royal Marines went on, I adapted to the introductory meeting at each posting, the regimented meet and greet. As we all do in any role, I became more confident but there were always so many different characters and you could never assume, become lazy or cocky!

The commanding officer needed to know his unit, their skills, strengths and any weaknesses. As my career progressed in the Royal Marines, I was in this position, meeting new officers. I then appreciated the importance of knowing your team; as individuals and as a unit. It was about functionality, safety and productivity but importantly, it was about respect. Mutual respect.

In Plymouth, I trained to be a chef. I had all the skills if I was required elsewhere but it was good to cook. As we used to always say, "You're a Royal Marine first," any positions you may take on are in addition to this fundamental training and primary role.

After my time in Plymouth, I was posted to Poole in Dorset and then Arbroath, 45 Commando in Scotland. In addition to this, I was posted during my time in the Royal Marines to the West Indies, Gibraltar and the Mediterranean, America, the South Pacific and Norway. I got to travel the world and have beautiful memories. Whilst training in Norway, I met and married a Norwegian lady. However, my training ended in Norway and returned to the UK. During this time I left the Royal Marines for a year before re-joining.

Unfortunately, over time and with the pressures of travelling as part of the job, the marriage failed. It was amicable and there was no malice but we drifted apart and the intimacy was gone. There weren't the communication techniques like there are today; the internet and mobile phones. Keeping long-distance relationships happy and healthy was much more of a challenge. We couldn't keep the connection and over time, the relationship ended, like a tree losing its final leaf in winter, after clinging on. I am certain now that we would always be there for each other if needed. This was my second marriage, having previously married a local woman, from North Shields, in 1980. She had joined me whilst I was in the military and we lived in married quarters. Our beautiful daughter, Ingha Mai, was born in 1982.

I have some great memories of my time in the Royal Marines. Memories evoke a myriad of emotions. Memories that are like the weather; a beautiful rainbow or a disastrous storm. Some things that can't be talked about, some things I bury deep but won't ever forget. Some things still make me smile fondly and laugh out loud and some things I'm not sure others would even truly understand.

A story that still makes me chuckle happened one night. I remember we were on board a ship and our team was all sleeping together in a small quarter. One oppo (crew) snored so loud he made a building site seem quiet. It became unbearable and we were all tired, emotionally and physically. He was on the top bunk and one night it became the itch that simply had to be scratched! So I pushed his bunk and even with the serial snorer on it, the bunk sprung up and folded into the bulkhead resulting in the serial snorer being sandwiched between the bunk and the cold wall. I had to shout for a teammate to quickly help me pull the bunk back down, releasing the trapped lad! But it definitely made for a quieter night's sleep after that. It was a harmless intention as we genuinely always had each other's back.

Me: on the right in 1993

There's a system in the Royal Marines called the Oppo system. It is effectively a buddy system, a 'you watch my back, I'll watch yours.' When you're in the forces, you are together all the time, there is no respite from each other. It's hard to adjust to when you first join but it's not up for negotiation and you become each other's shadows. It's different on civvy street. There isn't that deep level of connection, of support, of duty. Don't get me wrong, you have friends and people are still caring, but it's different in the forces. There is a level, a foundation level that everything else is built on. That no matter what, you have each other's back. There is no walking away, there's no giving up, it's not a choice. Like the air you breathe, your team is as essential to life. In civvy street, many don't care about their neighbour or the person in the street, it's sad. The forces are different. It's a family, even with the siblings who annoy you! The loyalty, the reliance, the unbreakable bond. It's what matters in every moment, but especially those critical ones. That unbreakable bond and that's what makes us the armed forces.

I became a sergeant in the Royal Marines and led my own team. The key to my leadership was respect. I respected my team and they respected me. This was fundamental to success as a full team. Hours, days and weeks could be hard and it was important to me that they knew they could knock at my door and that I would listen. We are all human and go through the same things. No one is immune, no one is different.

When I eventually left the Royal Marines, it was hard readjusting to civvy street. The mindset is different. The armed forces change you, in more ways than there are birds in the sky. You become part of a machine, a machine built with precision to defend and attack. You are a part of an engine that is needed to operate in any country of the world, at any time. Your identity becomes what it needs to become to function, to perform, in life and death situations. You have a value on life. When you leave that behind, you leave 99% of who you've become and need to find yourself again, deconstruct the machine and become someone who can exist in an unfamiliar world; civvy street.

I was lucky enough to get work when I left the Royal Marines in 1996. I had a job lined up, but had three months before I started. I lived out of a suitcase for a while, bouncing around in Scotland, before securing the job I held for many years. My role was working for a housing association, providing accommodation for veterans. This meant that I could support people who were like me, I would have a purpose and importantly, be around fellow armed forces folk.

The job was rewarding and important for my identity and readjustment to civvy street. In a way, it meant I didn't come home as a "Civvy," as I lived on site and the scheme felt like a community. I really enjoyed my time working there. When I retired from the post, I remained in Scotland for a while, only returning to the North East in the last year or so.

I have readjusted again and met lovely people. My health has deteriorated over the last few years and I rely on my family more. They support me and I still support them. We know our limits and boundaries. I need my privacy, just as they do. For much of my family's life, I have been at a distance, in the Royal Marines or in Scotland when I came back. It's readjustment for all. But it is wonderful to have them around and I have a beautiful granddaughter, Katie. My sisters, Heather and Christine are also a great support. It's nice to feel settled and to come to Operation Veteran each week. It means I'm around people who understand such an important and long part of my life. There's an unwritten rule, we will always help each other out. No two stories are ever the same, but we get it, we empathise and we understand life in the armed forces; the highs and the lows.

Dedicated to all members of the military who have served for Queen, King and country.

Afterword
Amy Kilty, Operation Veteran

I was working at a veteran accommodation service when I met Jim, from Operation Veteran. The organisation I was employed with invited him to a breakfast club. Jim came up with local veterans and the breakfast club was a great success. We then organised games nights together for the veterans which were equally as successful, if not fiercely competitive!

My contract ended not long after and I left the organisation. Whilst searching for permanent work, I began a temping job. Jim contacted me in December 2020, asking if I could do some work with Operation Veteran. I advised him I could do as much as needed whilst looking for a stable job. At this point, Jim had just secured the premises for Operation Veteran HQ. I went to visit and Jim explained there was a new vacant role, asking if I would be interested. It was part-time and with a mortgage to pay, it needed consideration. However, I was confident that it could be a great challenge and an amazing opportunity. I believed in everything Operation Veteran stood for and knew working with Jim would be great. I accepted the job and started in January 2021.

Funding increased over the last 18 months and now I work full-time for Operation Veteran as deputy business manager.

Operation Veteran is a phenomenal service that offers a plethora of support to veterans and their families across the area. We have a 'drop-in' for veterans to attend and a range of activities including a weekly wellbeing walk and breakfast club as well as a weekly lunch group. The door is always open for people to pop by and ask for advice. We have a network with other organisations to provide full support across any needs. Working closely with services offering substance misuse support, housing support, benefits advice, health and wellbeing and older person support. We reach out to partner organisations if we can't help, making sure the veteran is at the centre and ensuring their voice is heard.

Weekly, we have services such as Age UK North Tyneside, and Morrisons Community Champions as regulars at our headquarters during our weekly 'drop-in.' We pride ourselves on an environment where people are welcome, feel at ease and aren't judged. Sometimes a chat and a cuppa mean the world.

We also run a coffee shop that is open to the general public. Making all food on-site, we make produce tasty and affordable, using local suppliers. Our customers are very supportive and it means so much to us all.

We are funded by a range of charities including Veterans Foundation and the National Lottery Community Fund. We couldn't run our much-needed services without the generous funding, which allows us to provide all our veteran-specific services for free. We also have a part-time support worker who will be starting with the team soon and have a brilliant volunteer, George.

Operation Veteran is lovely to be a part of. Our veterans are such an important group in our society. They have given up part of their lives for our country; whether it be a day, a year or decades. It's amazing to be able to give something back to them. Seeing the veterans engage with  the Veterans' Voices project has been incredible. Hearing them talking about their own stories and the excitement of thinking people will read them has been magical. They don't think they are special people and that makes them even more special. Their stories are inspiring, moving and I'm delighted they are being shared.

You stand and choose to remember,
Things that so many of us wish we could
    forget.
Whilst in your quiet two-minute silence,
So many of us have our silence invaded with
    flashbacks and nightmares.
As you stand tall, proud of this nation's heroes,
So many of us can only sit, wrapped in guilt
    and pain.
Because the war doesn't end when you leave
    the battlefield,
A new fight begins inside your head.
So today, as you stand and choose to remember
    those that have fallen,
Think also of those that didn't fall,
But for who are now falling.

— Heather Perkins, 2013

Acknowledgments

Thank you for reading Veterans' Voices. I hope it took you on an emotional and educational journey and I hope the strangers in this book feel a little more like friends. If you enjoyed the book, please review it on Amazon and Goodreads. This helps raise awareness of the anthology and it's wonderful to read a review, thank you.

Veterans' Voices was only made possible by the kind donation from The National Lottery Community Fund and the support from Toni Clark at The Business Factory, North Tyneside. Thank you both so much.

Of course, there would be no book without the inspiring, wonderful folk at Operation Veteran, who in a very short time, I have become extremely attached to. Thank you to all the voices who made this project one of the best experiences of my life, I've learnt so much including that I'm a bigger softie than I thought!

Thank you to Jim, the director of Operation Veteran, who let me do my writer thing and always provided cuddles, encouragement and cuppas. Thank you to Amy for rounding up the troops to chat with a stranger, who I hope became a trusted person.

Massive thanks to my beloved Paul, who is my constant support and number one fan. Thank you for always being the first to read my work, believing in me and helping with so much.

Thank you to Bob (senecaauthorservices.com) for his wonderful cover design and book formatting support, over 4,000 miles away in Florida. Your kindness and belief in the project meant the world.

Thank you to Joanne for her brilliant eagle-eye editing and thank you to Donna for giving advice when the idea for Veterans' Voices was just a possibility.

Thank you to Write on the Tyne's non-executive directors, Alison and Caroline, for their crucial support.

Many thanks to Stellium Data Centres (stelliumdc.com) who generously sponsored the print and distribution of copies of Veterans' Voices, allowing all participants to have a copy and for the book to be gifted to local services and libraries. We appreciate you supporting our local community.

The biggest thanks to the veterans, whose stories have made a permanent stamp on my heart and who have nourished my world in such a short time. You truly are heroes.

Write on the Tyne (CIC) aims to make creative writing and expression inclusive to all. The company delivers a range of creative writing courses to groups in their community, helping to get everyone's voice heard. Write on the Tyne also produces commissioned written pieces to raise awareness, educate and help marginalised groups be heard.

Helen Aitchison is the director of Write on the Tyne. Published author of *The Dinner Club* and upcoming novel, *The Life and Love (Attempts) of Kitty Cook* (signed with Cahill Davis Publishing), Helen spent 20 years working in health and social care before establishing Write on the Tyne in May 2022.

Printed in Great Britain
by Amazon

18212691R00154